# N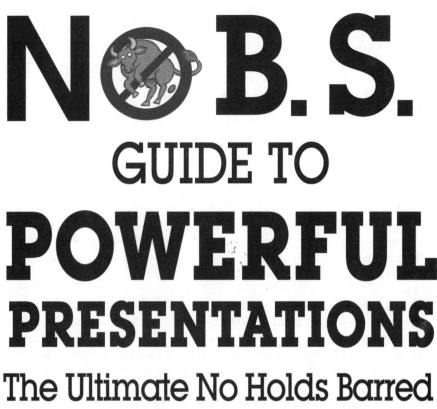B.S.

## GUIDE TO

# POWERFUL

# PRESENTATIONS

## The Ultimate No Holds Barred Plan to SELLING ANYTHING with Webinars, Online Media, Speeches, and Seminars

**BY**

## DAN S. KENNEDY & DUSTIN MATHEWS

**WITH**

DAVE VANHOOSE, GEOFF RONNING, AND MIKE CROW

Entrepreneur
PRESS®

⊘ W9-ADX-482

Publisher: Entrepreneur Press
Cover Design: Andrew Welyczko
Production and Composition: Eliot House Productions

This publication is designed to provide accurate and authoritative
information in regard to the subject matter covered. It is sold with the
understanding that the publisher is not engaged in rendering legal,
accounting or other professional services. If legal advice or other expert
assistance is required, the services of a competent professional person
should be sought.

**Library of Congress Cataloging-in-Publication Data**
Names: Kennedy, Dan S., 1954– author. | Mathews, Dustin.
Title: No B.S. guide to powerful presentations: the ultimate no
    holds barred plan to sell anything with webinars, online media,
    speeches, and seminars / Dan S. Kennedy, Dustin Mathews.
Description: Irvine: Entrepreneur Press, 2017. | Series: No B.S.
Identifiers: LCCN 2017003859 | ISBN 978-1-59918-607-8 (paperback)
    | ISBN 1-59918-607-1
Subjects: LCSH: Sales presentations. | Business presentations. |
    BISAC: BUSINESS & ECONOMICS / Business Communication /
    Meetings & Presentations. | BUSINESS & ECONOMICS / Skills.
    | BUSINESS & ECONOMICS / Entrepreneurship.
Classification: LCC HF5438.8.P74 K46 2017 | DDC 658.85—dc23
LC record available at https://lccn.loc.gov/2017003859

Printed in the United States of America

21  20  19  18  17                    10 9 8 7 6 5 4 3 2 1

# Contents

SECTION III

## FOLLOW-UP TO PRESENTATIONS

# Can One Great Presentation Change Everything for Your Business?

## Make You Rich? Influential? Powerful?

### by Dan Kennedy

W hat's the saying? Women want him and men want to be like him.

Having a powerful presentation, stepping to a stage or being on video, and delivering that presentation effectively can change a lot of things, for a person and for that person's business. It can do something even bigger . . .

*President* Donald J. Trump.

If you can look at it as an object lesson, objectively, you know that this is an unprecedented political/marketing miracle. It has many convergent, causative factors, including his opponent. But central to President Trump's h-u-g-e-l-y successful destruction of virtually every norm and believed requirement of campaigning was his mastery of powerful presentations. The Trump rallies were brilliantly organized and choreographed events with his own presentation as centerpiece. Were it not for his very deliberate effectiveness at delivering his presentations, he would not be the 45th President of the United States. And make no mistake, his presentations differed significantly from normal campaign speeches in a number of important ways. That specific analysis is being done by others and might be done by me in a different place at a different time. I raise it here only to set the stage for this book as demonstration of what the ability to craft and deliver a truly powerful presentation can do or be—virtually unlimited, altering or upsetting an entire industry or order, even putting an improbable President into the White House. Surely, there is a powerful presentation to be crafted and presented by you, capable of achieving whatever your chief purpose may be.

Comparatively, few owners of Main Street brick-and-mortar businesses—the butchers, bakers, and candlestick makers of the world—ever figure this out, develop a powerful presentation about what they do, and use it to attract customers. But the ones who do often find profound competitive advantage and accomplish amazing things. As an example, Tom and Nick Karadza have built a hugely profitable real estate brokerage in Toronto specializing in selling homes as investments to novice and pro investors, and they have built that business on the strength of powerful presentations delivered in their office to prospect audiences, online, and at larger seminars filled by their own advertising. Comparatively, few private practice professionals like chiropractors, dentists, child psychologists, lawyers, CPAs, and investment advisors ever figure this out, develop a powerful presentation about what they do, and use it to attract patients or clients, but the ones who do often find profound competitive advantage and accomplish amazing things. Matt Zagula, my co-author of the *No B.S. Guide to Trust-Based Marketing,* has a seven-figure-income financial practice in a painfully small market that has been fueled by "Evening with the Author" events and his powerful presentations at those events. Similarly, a private client of mine in the same field, James Lange, uses seminars on varied financial subjects to fuel his practice. Dr. Westermeier has mastered the use of in-office seminars on "Better Living with Dental Implants" marketed through his patients to their family members and friends. His presentation works so well and his system for marketing his in-office seminars is so effective, he has wound up with a second business licensing it to dentists all across the country. People in virtually *every field* are enjoying outsized incomes, immunity from price commoditization, attraction of better caliber customers, and strong competitive advantage by owning and using their own powerful group presentations and selling one to many instead of one to one. There are relatively few in every field, in every market. But they are thriving, and you can too.

That's why you're here, isn't it? You have come to the right place.

I poured rocket fuel into my own businesses and fortune with one powerful presentation delivered more than 400 times over nine years to an aggregate audience exceeding 3 million people. Doing so created direct revenues exceeding $1 million a year, and it was the chief builder of a company I later sold for tens of millions of dollars. It also was a media platform and subscription membership that supported me very well for over 25 years, and to some extent still does. Within that business, many powerful, million-dollar-producing presentations were and continue to be crafted and delivered live to audiences, online in webcasts and multi-piece VSLs (video sales letters) leading up to live webcasts, and by audio CDs and DVDs. You can look in on that business as it lives today at http://GKIC.com. It all came to life because of the one powerful presentation and my ability to deliver it as speaker/performer.

Can *one* great presentation make you rich? Absolutely.

That was so for me, personally. I've also helped conceive, craft, and write powerful presentations presented via half-hour TV infomercials that have, in total, driven billions—with a B—of dollars of revenue and built brands worth billions. I've helped individuals get powerful presentations together and master their delivery to, in turn, raise their or their business's prominence, promote their cause or charity, and make themselves famous as authors or experts. If you are going to establish yourself with the Triangle of Power that I use and teach—Authority, Credibility, and Celebrity—an essential item is a book, and the second essential item is a presentation.

Can *one* great presentation launch, fuel, and build an entire company? Absolutely.

In B2B, creating and delivering powerful presentations can make a huge difference. The leader in marketing management software for diverse small businesses and midsized companies in which I'm a founding investor, Infusionsoft (www. infusionsoft.com), was launched and built by several different presentations delivered first by their CEO and his partner, then by other speakers representing the company. Another "Planet Dan" company, 3DMailResults (http://3DMailResults. com), is the leading provider of ad specialties, promotional products, "lumpy mail" items and complete mailing campaigns utilizing such items. It has been fueled by Travis Lee's dynamic presentation that teaches and demonstrates the "why" and the "how" of using this kind of direct mail. My client Jay Geier launched what is now one of, if not, the largest training and consulting companies in dentistry, Scheduling Institute, with one great presentation about the right and wrong handling of incoming calls in dental offices. Today, the company has two physical campuses—in Atlanta and Phoenix—conducts over a thousand trainings in dental offices each year, and is an enormously valuable enterprise. Just as Walt always reminded folks that "it all started with a mouse," this all started with a presentation, delivered to audiences of dentists.

Can *one* presentation give an ordinary business an extraordinary advantage? Absolutely.

At the Main Street, local level, one great speech can differentiate a doctor, lawyer, financial advisor, school operator, restaurant owner, real estate agent, etc., etc., from all competitors and peers and make them a leading expert and famous celebrity in their market. Years back, a client of mine, David Apts, fueled exceptionally profitable physical therapy clinics with his Back Safety class, delivered regularly to the employees of the factories, coal plants, and other industrial companies in his area, in their workplaces. This pre-empted all other practitioners for all these workers' compensation cases. This somewhat replicated a system that a partner and I had invented for selling large quantities of Mace®-like chemical deterrent key chains and other self-defense products by sending speakers into all sorts of companies and offices to conduct free Crime Safety classes. Even stores like Home Depot® drive sales with in-store classes for customers. Yes, this requires some creative imagination. But the genesis for it is there: If your business has customers, that means that some presentation related to what people do with what they buy from your business will have an audience. And you can safely bet that if you figure this out and run with it, your close competitors won't.

At the national level, one great presentation delivered via online video, entirely automated, can circumvent normal distribution channels, sell direct to consumers, and be a self-operating income machine. One of these that I created for a client nine years ago has put money in his bank account every day of its life, all the way to the present, untouched by human hands, while he spends a lot of his time on his boat. Think about how happy he is, each month placing one call to his mailing house and directing them to mail 10,000, 25,000, or 50,000 of his direct-mail pieces, letting those mailings bring his audience to his automated webinar, and getting daily email verifications of orders processed and the daily bank deposit made. This isn't freakish or fantasy. It is very doable with what you'll discover in this bookin addition to the resources it recommends.

If you want to see one fine-tuned presentation after another enabling inventors, manufacturers, and entrepreneurs to bypass all traditional sales distribution channels and barriers, tune into the home shopping TV channels QVC and HSN for a few days or at least a few hours. You will see baked goods, steaks, candy, and all sorts of food items, home and business gadgets, fashion, jewelry, gardening tools, you-name-it sold by powerful presentations and by individuals—usually the baker, the rancher, the candy maker, the inventor, the designer, the person behind the brand—delivering them. My friend and client, the late Joan Rivers, was, for years, the number-one sales presenter on QVC, which attached to an ever-expanding portfolio of products bearing her name. She was not winging it. Each product's presentation was crafted to be a powerful presentation.

This book is about that craftsmanship.

In this book, I've partnered with my friend Dustin Mathews, who heads up a remarkable agency and its team, a quasi-factory with a quasi-assembly line, for creating powerful, leverageable presentations for businesspeople of every imaginable type 'n' stripe, hundreds of times every year. He starts with the raw material of an individual's life, interests, stories, experiences, nature of his business or profession, and, of course, his objectives at one end of the assembly line. At the other end, instead of a shiny new car driving off, a shiny new power presentation comes off—with script, MS PowerPoint® slides, other visual aids, video media, or whatever else is needed for it to be used successfully for influence, promotion, or profit. In short, he has refined an art to a system, and, just as Henry Ford made the motorcar affordable for the masses by his assembly line, Dustin has made developing and owning power presentations affordable for just about anyone, whether entrepreneur, professional, author, or expert. From his constant, daily experience with moving one person after another through his process, he has settled on certain conclusions, principles, strategies, structures, modes of storytelling, and sales tactics that are reliable "best practices" for creating power presentations as a do-it-yourselfer—for any purpose—even one-time-use purposes like a Monday morning staff meeting or a specific presentation to your corporate board. As many as you need, as often as you need them.

To return to President Trump for a moment . . .

He created what Dave VanHoose explains in this book is a Signature or Stadium Presentation. He assembled target-selected audiences to deliver it to, and multiplied its reach beyond those in-person events with media. His presentation can be dissected by Dustin Mathews' presentation formulas. If following this can put an unlikely candidate into the White House, what might it do for you?

Let's find out . . .

---

## Important Invitation

You do not need to wait until you've read the book to connect with its authors for additional free resources, information, and more!

Dustin Mathews and Dave VanHoose are at www.SpeakingEmpire.com and extensions of this book are at http://NoBSPresentations.com.

Dan Kennedy's newsletters, association for marketing-oriented entrepreneurs, and a wide range of resources based on his methods can be found and accessed at http://GKIC.com.

There is a special offer from GKIC on page 165.

---

# PUTTING TOGETHER YOUR MOST POWERFUL PRESENTATION

# CHAPTER 1

# Will You Be an Amateur or a Pro?

by Dan Kennedy

"All *the world's a stage* ..." *wrote* Shakespeare, *who* made his living creating presentations for people to perform.

We make our way through life creating and delivering presentations.

In your mind, you play out how you will ask her out for a date, how you'll propose, how you'll have "the talk" with your son, how you'll take the car keys away from your father—then you deliver these presentations. You imagine your presentations to your boss, your associates, your board of directors, your clients before you deliver them. Most people only do this: imagine, deliver. A small percentage of people choose to put a lot more into this as a process—conception, preparation, refinement, practice, delivery. We have a term for these people: *professionals*. You get to decide whether to be an amateur or a professional about this activity that controls so much of your life.

It's worth noting that amateurs aren't well paid.

Fortunately, I was introduced to *the concept of presentation* very early in my business life. By that I mean, I understood that just about everything we get or achieve is the result of effectively delivering effective presentations. This led me to the realization that most people were not conscious of this and even if they were, they were not strategic and deliberate about it. To the contrary, they were random. In this, I recognized the possibility for advantage, and at the time, I sorely needed to find some advantage, because I had plenty of disadvantages. So I became a very serious student of the architecture, engineering, craftsmanship, and writing of winning presentations.

I've never stopped studying it. One of the first books I found was titled *Dynamic Selling* by S. Robert Tralins. The hardcover edition I got at a used bookstore in 1971 was published in 1961. At the time, I was still in high school, and I was selling a hodge-podge of things to homeowners and to small-business people, basically door to door. Following the instructions and examples in that book, I sat down and, for the first time, wrote out my presentations, in paragraphs, on 4" x 6" cards. I organized and reorganized them. I rewrote them. I refined it all and got it, as I teach on this now, "tight and right." I immediately got better results. What I found in that book was very primitive and simplistic compared to what you are about to find in this one. But both it and this book focus on structure. That alone was enough to make a significant difference, and I wondered how much better results I could get from presentations and how much better I could get as a presenter—or, more descriptively, a performer of presentations—if every aspect was identified and improved.

Structure is important. An excellent, modern book on this is Michael Masterson's *The Architecture of Persuasion: How to Write Well-Constructed Sales Letters*. But, as with virtually every kind of success, there is no one thing behind it. In fact, the lust for *the* one thing, *the* magic pill, *the* secret ingredient is what dooms most people to frustration and recurring failure with just about anything they attempt—from losing weight and keeping it off, to golfing, to making and delivering effective presentations, to putting their ideas across, to influencing and leading, or to outright selling goods or services. So I drew from many sources to develop a complex, sophisticated approach to crafting effective presentations and to performing them as a presenter. I'll tell you about much of this throughout this book. I drew from diverse and eclectic sources. Most importantly, I made myself *very* deliberate.

Let me summarize the results of this for me. I became a star salesman, and I have literally sold my way through life. I became a professional speaker, paid to speak, earning upwards from $1 million a year from speaking engagements and seminars for many years, including nine consecutive years as one of only two permanent players on the largest seminar stages and tour America has ever seen, with audiences of 10,000 to 35,000, in sports arenas. By speaking, I fueled development of a company that has since sold twice and a spin-off of that company that has grown very large, all of which made me rich. I created a reputation and a personal brand that has stood me in good stead for four decades and permits my conducting all my business on my terms with enormous autonomy. I even became a much sought after and highly paid writer and crafter of sales presentations and scripts for speakers, for TV infomercials, for online sales videos and webcasts, and for presentations in other media. My fees and royalties routinely run from $100,000.00 to $250,000.00 for one of these projects.

For all this, I have been self-educated, meaning no courses, instructors, mentors. Had I found something comparable to my co-author's system for crafting presentations and his "incubator" where people come and craft great presentations with his team in a super-condensed time period, I believe I would have gotten to good, then great, and ultimately my greatest results much sooner, with a lot less time spent figuring it out. I was like Lewis and Clark making my way through wilderness and creating my own trail. They have a road map, templates, plug-'n'-play structure, and the experience of having helped hundreds of clients and thousands of students use their tools.

If you don't own one, I'm sure you've seen the whiz-bang juicers demonstrated on TV. Into one, the person puts a cantaloupe, a head of lettuce, a carrot, an apple, and a fish, and maybe a brick for good measure, and out the other end comes an incredibly condensed, nutrition-rich juice. That's what Dustin Mathews and his partner Dave VanHoose have done with all the ingredients of effective presentations. He's built a juicer. Further, he's developed a community for people committed to success as presenters called Speaking Empire. Throughout this book, Dustin offers windows to this world, online, and I hope you'll take advantage of all of them.

What I can tell you with absolute certainty is this: Willie Shakespeare got it nearly right. *All* the world's a stage. *Most* people are merely players. Relatively few people are its masters. To them, the world hands over any bounty asked of it.

In Willie's day, the stage consisted only of the physical stage. Today, media is as much the main stage as is the physical environment—land, sea, office, and home. Being able to conceive and craft presentations for media, from four-minute videos to four-hour webcasts, from 140-character tweets to 4,000-word online sales letters, is now *critically* important. There are few captive audiences for anybody or anything, so knowing how to captivate and control an audience is of paramount importance.

Powerful presentations and being able to present them have always been keys to extraordinary success, rising far above peers and competitors. Thomas Edison. Steve Jobs. Separated by a vast span of time but sharing these same two great differentiators.

The foundation of success hasn't changed: message, media, market, i.e., audience. The level of sophistication you can bring to this triangle keeps advancing and advancing and advancing. It's really no place or time for amateurs. Make up your mind to be a pro.

CHAPTER 2

# How To Be Fearless
## as a Presenter

by Dustin Mathews

S ince Dale Carnegie first brought "public speaking" front and center in the American consciousness in 1912— making executives and entrepreneurs aware that success or failure in their careers or businesses might hinge on their willingness and ability to stand up and speak to groups about their ideas—a somewhat surprising fact has been verified and re-verified by poll after poll after poll: More people fear doing this than fear snakes, heights, debilitating illness, even death. I totally get this.

When I first set foot on the campus of Florida State University, I was filled with optimism. It would only take a day before I was scared out of my mind. I discovered that, to graduate, I would have to take a course in public speaking.

The minute I walked into that classroom, my fear intensified and my heart rate skyrocketed. The classroom was set up like a mini-stadium, with stacked rows of seats that seemed to rise into infinity. Just the roar of 300 students in pre-class conversations was enough to make me want to shut the door behind me—and run!

I stayed, only to next hear the professor telling us we would each write and deliver ten different speeches over the course of the semester, some to the entire class of 300, some to smaller groups.

I am a technical guy. In fact, I was in school to get a degree in computer science. Having to "perform" was not for me. I'd like to tell you I had the courage to stay put, but I slinked away. I hoped to find a smaller class or a less demanding professor. When the next semester rolled around, I found myself with no choice but to enroll in the class again. When I opened the door, I found the same stadium, the same 300, the same professor. I again made myself disappear.

I next went to a lot of trouble to find a loophole. I found it by chasing a girl . . . right into an extracurricular class she was taking called Model United Nations. If you took that, you could exempt yourself from the requisite public speaking class. I didn't get the girl, but I did graduate without ever having to stand up in front of those 300 other students and speak.

Fast forward a few years . . .

My business partner Dave VanHoose said, "Dustin, I'm not going to be able to give tonight's presentation. You're going to have to do it." A lot of money was at stake. A commitment by our company. There was no loophole.

I did what I had to do. And I experienced something amazing. I was a 20-year-old kid talking to older men and women with more life experience, about investing in foreclosure real estate, put forward as an expert. I realized that people looked at me differently just because I was standing up in front of them and speaking. I realized that just being on that stage and delivering my presentation completely changed my position with those people and their perception of me. It gave me instant authority and credibility, despite my age. I also experienced something else equally amazing. My sense of self changed. Stepping way outside my "comfort zone" and doing something I'd avoided for so long raised my confidence level about everything I was doing.

> *Being able to build and deliver effective presentations has practical benefits—you can more efficiently sell whatever it is you sell or promote whatever business or professional practice you own, you can speed up a business's growth, you can use yourself as ad media—but it also has personal benefits.*

Most of our clients report very similar experiences. Whether or not they have already been speaking and making presentations, when they really understand and use the *science* of effective presentations, they not only get better results but also they feel better about themselves. Dan Kennedy says that "Competence Creates Confidence," and that trying to mentally manufacture confidence without feeling knowledgeable and competent about it is nearly impossible. Fear is best erased by actually knowing what you are doing and why you are doing it as you are. It is easier to create calm confidence with a strong sense of having and following a reliable blueprint for what you are doing than by psychological and motivational tricks. You don't have to trick yourself into temporary fearlessness about a journey to an unfamiliar destination if you possess a reliable map or GPS, and an equally reliable vehicle.

Most people don't know that there is a *formula* for creating and for delivering powerful presentations. Most of the fears surrounding speaking—whether to 10 in a boardroom, or 50 at a seminar to get patients or clients or customers for a small business, or 500 as an author or professional speaker—are basically fears of the unknown. My first goal for this book is to help you replace any fears you have about making presentations with a confidence based on formula and process. This is the result of years of helping executives, entrepreneurs, authors, representatives of charities, and others gain both the practical and personal benefits of stepping to the front of a room and confidently, capably delivering a powerful presentation, making sure that when you open the door at the back and see 300 people milling about, you won't want to close the door behind you— and run!

# CHAPTER 3

# Knowledge of Your Audience
## Is Power

by Dan Kennedy

L ike Dustin, early on, I was scared. Very early on, I also stuttered and had to fight to control that. I totally understand the impulse to flee. Like Dustin, early on, I started stepping to the fronts of rooms and giving presentations under duress—not by desire. Even as I got good at it at one level, trepidation returned as I moved to different levels. The first time I peered through a curtain into a basketball arena and saw 15,000 people there, soon to have *me* come out from behind that curtain, I briefly wondered if I was up to it. I subsequently appeared on that event tour over 230 times in as many as 27 cities a year for 9 consecutive years and never felt trepidation about it after those first few minutes. By then, I had—as arrogant as it may sound—mastered two kinds of knowledge-producing know-how that provided more than enough competence for more than enough confidence.

One of those knowledge sets was the architecture for powerful presentations: the script. Its order, its language, its ebb and flow. The best mix of exposition, assertion, story, humor, and more. In this book, I'm leaving most of the discussion up to Dustin.

The other set of knowledge I'd learned to acquire and use was Audience Knowledge.

**When a presentation lands *a direct hit* on an audience's interests, beliefs, doubts, fears, hopes, ambitions, pre-existing ideas, pre-existing self-talk, its acceptance and enthusiasm for you as the presenter skyrockets and expands, and it is nearly impossible to fail.** In fact, you are given more credit than your actual performance may deserve. When you know who the people in your audience are, what their lives are all about, what their daily experiences are, what their deepest-seated emotions are, you can make sure the presentation you assemble and deliver lands one direct hit after another after another. I previously mentioned President Trump. He is President largely because of this. He really, really, really knew his target audience, crafted presentations that landed direct hits, and delivered them with the confidence that comes out of that certain knowledge.

**What is a direct hit?** It is an idea, assertion, single sentence, or single story that is *precisely and exactly* in sync with the audience hearing it. As an example, anytime I talk to entrepreneurs about being the lone polar bear in a forest of grizzlies, and then talk about their sense of isolation and loneliness, of being underappreciated and disrespected, of being negatively labeled (workaholic, greedy, evil 1%'er, etc.), I land a direct hit. When

I first heard Zig Ziglar talk to "lowly" salespeople about being in "THE Proud Profession," being the unsung heroes of the entire economy, the engine on which everything and everyone depended, and as improving lives for a living, I recognized he was landing a direct hit. I've borrowed that entire idea for my own presentation, books, newsletters, and dialogue with salespeople. When I first heard Trump roll out "Make America Great AGAIN," I knew that—especially with that fourth word— he landed a very direct hit on the leading-edge boomer and senior audience that I wrote about extensively in my book *No B.S. Guide to Marketing to Boomers and Seniors.*

My speaking colleague, the famous success philosopher Jim Rohn, actually made his main, generic presentation on personal development from his specific version of it for multi-level/network marketing distributors. That presentation landed direct hits with all audiences of salespeople and small-business people, particularly those struggling to get ahead and struggling with their own emotions and behaviors. Jim had them, as the cliché goes, eating out of the palm of his hand. Yet Jim was not the charismatic, super-forceful presenter that Trump was at his campaign rallies. Jim was a calmer, more cerebral, more thoughtful, somewhat professorial (but never condescending), paternal teacher. Jim was not "perfect" on stage either, as "perfect" might well have been insisted on in the college speech class Dustin avoided. Jim would even turn his back to his audiences to write and draw on a giant chalkboard or marker board. Jim was, however, every bit as effective as Trump in connecting because he deeply understood his audiences.

I have my own somewhat odd "style" for being on stage and delivering presentations. It would likely have gotten me a big, red "F" in that college speaking class. It works for me. But what makes it work, or maybe allows for it to work, is my deep and thorough understanding of my audiences. For 40 years, I've gone out of my way to create and deliver presentations to audiences I am certain I have intimate understanding of. I believe I can recite for you, verbatim, the late night, kitchen table conversation that occurs in their homes, when one can't sleep and comes downstairs and the other notices his or her absence from the marital bed and follows. I believe I can recite for you, verbatim, that person's major, recurring conversations with himself that he has as he drives his car to and from work.

From about 1979 to 1983, I spoke to a lot of chiropractic and dental groups. Some of these doctors who first saw and heard me then, in small groups of 30 to 100, or on a few occasions at large events of 1,000 to 3,000, are still with me today, as newsletter subscribers, members of the GKIC organization (http: //GKIC. com), and even attending seminars where I speak—34 to 38 years later! It's important to understand I am not and never was a chiropractor or a dentist, never worked in any capacity in such practices, and cannot adjust your back or drill your tooth. But by my presentations to these audiences alone, I have generated at least $20 million in direct revenue, plus countless lifelong customers of considerable value. For these same audiences/ markets, I have written and developed presentations for 18 different clients who all sell various goods and services, and these, combined, have generated much more revenue. One such presentation is the genesis of a $30-million-per-year business, likely worth at least $150 million if and when it is sold. How is all this possible without having been a DC or DDS?

You don't have to be one of a particular population in order to develop thorough knowledge about that population, how they think, what they feel, and what they truly, deeply want. I am assured there are even men who have developed this level of knowledge about women and that there are women who have done so about men. I've never met such an expert, but that doesn't mean they don't exist. First of all, a certain amount of human nature, psychology, and reactive behavior is either hardwired or deeply embedded in early childhood, by about age ten. This is universal, to all groups, and can be used in embedding "triggers" into presentations that audiences can't resist responding to. Then, second, there are basic questions to ask and know answers to about any target market or audience, for any advertising, marketing, persuasion, or influence effort, regardless of how it is to be done. You'll find this "magic list" (Figure 3.1) below. Finally, third, there is the sense of a group to be gained by reading what they read, hanging out where they hang

**FIGURE 3.1:** The Magic Question List

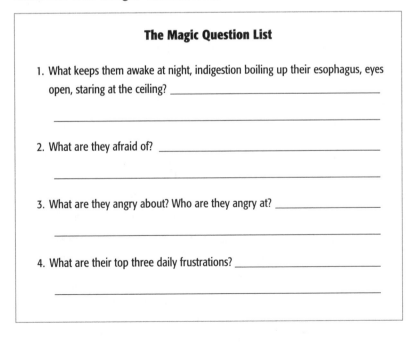

**The Magic Question List**

1. What keeps them awake at night, indigestion boiling up their esophagus, eyes open, staring at the ceiling? _____

   _____

2. What are they afraid of? _____

   _____

3. What are they angry about? Who are they angry at? _____

   _____

4. What are their top three daily frustrations? _____

   _____

FIGURE **3.1:** The Magic Question List, continued

---

**The Magic Question List**

5. What trends are occurring and will occur in their businesses or lives? _____

_____

6. What do they secretly, ardently desire most? _____

_____

7. Is there a built-in bias to the way they make decisions? (Example: engineers = exceptionally analytical) _____

_____

8. Do they have their own language? _____

_____

9. Who else is selling something similar to their product, and how? _____

_____

10. Who else has tried selling them something similar, and how has that effort failed? _____

_____

---

out, talking, listening, or playing anthropologist. For instance, a weekend at a boat show will give you a lot of knowledge about boating enthusiasts. From all this comes Audience Knowledge.

When I peered through that curtain at those 30,000 eyeballs and 30,000 ears, I reminded myself that the presentation I was going to walk out there and deliver was finely crafted and honed by Audience Knowledge. Out there were (mostly) small business and Main Street, brick-and-mortar business owners, more entrepreneurial businesspeople, people from direct-selling companies, and salespeople attached to very diverse products and services—but all having the same late-night kitchen table conversations. I had a presentation certain to land direct hits. With that Audience Knowledge as the foundation of my presentation, I could not fail.

# CHAPTER 4

# What IS a Presentation?

by Dan Kennedy

When we talk about crafting and delivering a maximum-effectiveness presentation, it's good to have clarity about what the thing is that we're building.

There is the old story of four or five blindfolded men led to different parts of an elephant. The one wrapping his arms around a leg thinks he's found a gigantic tree trunk. The one touching the trunk thinks he's got the tail of a King Kong-size horse. And so on.

Let's be sure you're not blindfolded, groping, and guessing.

A presentation is, above all else, a means to an end. For businesspeople and sales professionals, it can be the equivalent of other advertising media used to establish brand identity, consumer awareness, or more directly, to attract and acquire customers. It can be a means of making an actual sale, whether one-to-one or one-to-many. But it is not anything unique. It is a means to an end in the same way an airplane flight is a means of getting to a destination or a shovel is a means of getting a hole dug. Don't assign any uniqueness or mysticism to it.

Because it is a means to an end, the desired outcome has to govern everything leading up to that desired outcome. You start with the outcome in mind, and you never start crafting a presentation without the end in mind. It may or may not surprise you that many people err with this. They begin at the beginning. They have some opportunity arise to make a presentation, or they have the notion of giving presentations for their business, and they dive into crafting the presentation. How to open? What stories or jokes to tell? What information to dispense? The right place to start is with the desired outcome. These other questions then become: How should I open the presentation in a way that sets up and facilitates my desired outcome? What stories should I tell that set up and facilitate the desired outcome?

If you are crafting a presentation for a specific purpose, to achieve a specific desired outcome, you are deprived of creative liberty. You are not an artist, free to throw any color paint you like in any pattern or arrangement you like onto a blank canvas. You do not get to choose your opening remarks, your stories, your jokes, your key points, your information, or the order it all gets put into. You relinquish all that liberty to your desired outcome.

I come from a background in advertising. Civilians and amateurs mistakenly think of advertising as a creative exercise, and I initially imagined that this was the case. In the advertising industry, peer-to-peer awards are often given to the most creative ads. But this is not the reality of *good* advertising at all. One of the all-time legendary leaders of the advertising world, David Ogilvy, said, "In advertising, creativity is what sells." I carried this with me into my speaking and my crafting of presentations. For me, a great presentation was and is, by definition, one that successfully sells. Every item and element in a great presentation is put there because it serves and facilitates that purpose. Because of that, a favorite story I love to tell and tell well is ruled out, and a different one I have no fondness for gets in. So it is with every line, every sentence, every idea, every story included in a presentation. This is a strict and rigid discipline.

A lot of people underestimate the value of discipline. For several years, on a multicity pubic seminar tour, the speaker preceding me was General Norman Schwarzkopf, made famous by directing Desert Storm, our march through Iraq to rescue Kuwait, under the first President Bush. Norm had a line: "Shined shoes save lives." By that, he meant that getting soldiers to be very disciplined about seemingly small things like having perfectly shined shoes every morning automatically carried over to being disciplined about big things, in the heat of battle, with bullets flying and bombs dropping all around them. I think a lot of people are worried and nervous about delivering a presentation to an audience and can be easily thrown off their game while presenting because there wasn't enough discipline about the crafting of the presentation to start with. They aren't confident in presenting because they lack confidence in their presentation. The more disciplined you are in your defining of presentation, and the preparation of your presentation, the better off you'll be when out there with bullets flying.

By common dictionary definition and thesaurus synonyms, a presentation can be a formal or official proffer of idea, information, or proposal for consideration; a demonstration; a performance. The best ones are all three of these things. A great presentation includes a specific proposition for which acceptance, agreement, and often, a purchase is asked for and obtained. That is the outcome governing everything. Very often, a great presentation includes some physical or evidentiary, even dramatic, demonstration that facilitates the audience's acceptance of the proposition, and every great presentation is delivered as a great performance. It is never just what is said, but also how it is said. With TV infomercials, I always test them with the sound muted; what "sense of this" is the audience getting just from the facial expressions, gestures, body language, and actions of the performers, making its way into their subconscious by visual intake, absent the words?

A maximum-effectiveness presentation is not just a means of conveying or communicating ideas or information, unless you are being paid as a professor or schoolteacher in a classroom. For our purposes, it is a means of seeking and hopefully gaining acceptance and agreement for ideas or information conveyed by it, leading to a purchase or other specific action. I would add, teachers who only convey ideas and information are relatively poorly paid, especially if compared to people who craft and deliver presentations that persuade people to buy.

The upshot of all this is that a maximum-effectiveness presentation is a purposed *thing*; that is far more scientific than it is creative. You might think of it as analogical to the blueprints prepared by an architect. There is a creative aspect to being an architect. But the blueprints ultimately have to be used to construct a house, and to wind up with a house that "works" for people who are going to live in it. The roof can't be designed so creatively that it leaks in every corner. The architect is severely limited in how he can indulge his creative impulses and preferences—by the practical purpose that must be achieved and by his client. In crafting a presentation, your client and your practical purpose are one and the same: the desired outcome.

In simple terms, this is more a pragmatic exercise than it is a creative one.

This gets us to formula.

Most disciplined, pragmatic activities have formulas. Architects, scientists, even novelists approach their work by formulas. It is very useful to do so. If, for example, I give you the task of making up and writing or telling a "great story," and turn you loose to do so, it's going to be very difficult to do. You'll probably draw on some personal experience or memory or that of somebody you know, but you might, instead, make one up out of pure imagination. Or you might "borrow" a classic fairy tale or novel's plot and try altering it enough to disguise the plagiarism. You'll make random decisions about the order of things in the story. You'll be at sea without navigation. But if I give you a copy of the book *The Writer's Journey: Mythic Structure for Writers* by Christopher Vogler, you'll have a formula, a structure, and an architecture for your entire story and for what writers call "the hero's journey." This alone will make your task infinitely easier.

Admittedly, this replaces true, pure art with paint-by-numbers, but it is important to remember that you are not an artist. You surrender your creative impulses to the desired outcome, and that makes paint-by-numbers very valuable and efficient. If you are going to become a master storyteller and a professional writer of presentations and a professional speaker, you will want to study these subjects in great depth and transcend paint-by-numbers and rigid formulas. By all means do so. I do not just own the above-referenced book on story structure and storytelling; I own, have studied, and frequently return to over 100 books just on that aspect of writing. But I do this as my chief occupation and have for 40 years. If you have another business—your insurance agency, your restaurant, your health-care practice—and you are using presentations as ad media, sales media, and promotional or public relations activities, you need a more serviceable approach.

In the next chapter, Dave VanHoose lays out the formula for crafting presentations that he and Dustin use most with clients in diverse businesses. It is, by its standardization, rigid, even arbitrarily rigid—very much a paint-by-numbers process. It is not the only way to craft presentations; it is easy and natural to argue against such rigidity. Yet it is that "one way" rigidity that provides high reliability.

That is, for me, and probably for you, the final defining point about a presentation: reliability. We want a presentation that produces its desired outcome within a small and tolerable range of variability, every time, every place, with every audience.

# CHAPTER 5

# The Speakers' Formula™

by Dave VanHoose

T here are certain things everybody needs to own. Every man should own a navy blue blazer. If you have an empty closet and hire a dress-for-success expert or a clothier or other knowledgeable advisor, one of the first things they'll have you buying is a navy blue blazer.

There are a lot of accepted necessities. Toothpaste comes to mind. Participating in civilized society has certain required necessities—for men, pants. What a lot of people don't understand is that *success* has certain required necessities, too.

We put together this book because all three of us believe that owning at least one highly effective presentation is a success essential, owning more than one—possibly for different media—is better, and owning the ability to craft additional ones as needed is best.

Everybody should own a Signature Presentation, which, at Speaking Empire, we sometimes call your Stadium Presentation, in tribute to the seating in that classroom my partner Dustin ran from.

This is a message that works for you no matter when, where, or how you share it—speaking, in a webcast or webinar, facing one person across a desk or 100 people from a stage. This becomes *the core* of any and every presentation you deliver. Our friend and co-author here, Dan Kennedy, has a portfolio of speeches about his *Magnetic Marketing*® system. They are 60, 75, 90, and 120 minutes in length. There is a generic one for audiences of varied kinds of business owners and salespeople, specific ones for single professions or businesses or sales groups—for real estate agents or for financial advisors, for example—and adaptations for delivery by other presenters such as GKIC.com's Certified Magnetic Marketing® Advisors, for video sales letters delivered online, and for sales letters delivered by mail (see https://GKIC. com). In all of these, the core is the same. Usually, we discover that our new clients lack clarity and certainty about their core, and this is one of the important things we help them work out.

Here's how I started learning the importance of this: When I started my first business, I believed it had to thrive and would be the most incredible business. With it, I was going to help people save time, energy, *and* money. What could be more attractive than that? So, like many startup entrepreneurs, I pulled out my credit cards and launched my business with a pile of personal debt. Guess how many customers flocked to me the first month? Right. Zero. Of course, I thought that I had such a great idea, the customers would come. A little panicked, I resorted to desperate and frenzied activity, with what I call the Six-Foot Rule: If anybody was within six feet of me, I tried to sell them. I quickly realized that selling to one person at a time, one after the other, with a high percentage rejecting me for one reason or excuse or another, was going to be incredibly difficult. It was inefficient. There was only one of me, and I could run only so fast, work so hard, and take so much rebuffing. I now know, by the way, that this causes a lot of people who enter various kinds of selling businesses or careers to fail, unnecessarily.

*Since there was just one of me and a whole lot of them to sort through, to get a customer, I asked myself: why am I speaking to them one at a time? Why don't I speak to a bunch of them together, at one time? This is now often called "one-to-many selling."*

I put together my first audience of prospects in the back room at a Denny's. I invited many, 12 showed up, I sold to 20% of them right then and there, and made about $2,000.00. It blew my mind. I might have sold to the same 20% meeting with each of the 12 one at a time, over coffee in a booth at that same Denny's, but it would have taken 12 hours instead of 2, I'd have been personally confronted and fatigued by each of the no's, and I'd have owed the waitress rent! Or I might not have even sold to 20%, because there is a group dynamic that helps sales, that never exists in person-to-person selling. From that point on, I concentrated on selling to groups, and for a while, I was speaking at a lunch and at a dinner every day, five days a week.

I was selling, right then and there. A lot of people we help with presentations are, instead, only selling follow-up, one-on-one appointments—like a dentist doing a seminar for invited patients about implants in his office, a CPA doing a lunch presentation for invited small-business owners about cutting taxes, or a travel agent speaking at a civic club about cruise vacations. It doesn't matter. The process is pretty much the same, and the benefits are absolutely the same.

The key is the Signature Presentation. If it works, you can do just about anything. You can switch from slow and frustrating one-to-one selling to efficient group selling, in your own office, in a restaurant's back room, once a month or twice a day.

Within three years of starting my first business with my credit cards, this switch in the way I sold made it the 35$^{th}$ fastest growing private company in America, placing on the Inc. 500 List!

Over time, at Speaking Empire, we have "locked in" a formula for these kinds of Signature Presentations, evolved from the one I used initially in the back room at Denny's. From acorns mighty oak trees grow!

As you can see in Figure 5.1, page 31, this Speaker's Formula™ organizes your presentation into 12 component parts, in a particular order. I say: Success loves sequence. There are, of course, any number of ways a top pro speaker might rearrange these components and add to or subtract from them, creating his own, preferred presentation sequence. *Maybe* with good reason. If you are not that top pro, rich with successful experience at crafting powerful presentations, I urge sticking with this Formula. Let's talk a little about each component . . .

## 1: Grab Attention

When most people get up on stage, make a video, or hold a webinar, they talk *at* people. That's a pushing energy. It actually pushes people away. It is better to draw them toward and into

FIGURE **5.1:** The Speaker's Formula™

your presentation so that they give you their attention and get interested in what you have to say. A compelling emotional or dramatic story can do this. This can tie to your reason for making your presentation and for being in the business or for selling the product you are selling. A set of provocative questions is another approach. A set of specific, intriguing promises is yet another. One way or another, the first block of your presentation needs to be about getting and holding attention.

## 2: Build Rapport

People buy from people they know, like, and trust. People don't just buy things from you; they have to *buy you*. An excellent way to build rapport is with personal transparency. You may choose to share your personal challenges, an obstacle you've overcome, or doubts you conquered that got you to this moment of appearing before your audience and introducing them to your opportunity. Dustin's story in Chapter 2 is this kind of a story. It is usually a mistake to barrel ahead with a presentation of facts, figures, product features and benefits, and propositions without first establishing some rapport with the audience.

## 3: Gain Credibility

An audience needs some reassurance that you deserve being listened to. The same presentation gets very different results if delivered by two different people and only one has and gives reasons why he has the right to talk about the subject and to talk to the audience in front of him. Are you part of a respected group or association? Are you an author? Have you been seen in relevant publications? Have you been seen on TV or heard on radio? Are you just another cosmetic surgeon, or are you THE cosmetic surgeon who wrote *The Official Consumer's Guide to Cosmetic Surgery* . . . who lectured at known hospitals . . . who has been a guest on a popular TV show . . . who is certified in the technique favored by major movie stars? In short, you need to lay out your claims to fame at this point in your presentation.

NO B.S. Guide to Powerful Presentations 🎙 33

If you do not have any of this now, getting it is one of the many things we assist Speaking Empire clients with, in addition to the development of their Signature Presentation.

## 4: Target Problems

Your audience entered the room, came to the webinar, started listening to your audio CD already in and with pain—if not physical, then in the broader sense: disappointment, frustration, recurring failure, anxiety, confusion. *Everybody* has something of this nature going on. For many people, it is simmering—not acute or urgent. At this point in your presentation, you want to draw it out and state it, turn up its heat, and make it acute and urgent. Relatively few people can be motivated by gain alone. Most move toward gain as a way of escaping pain.

## 5: Deliver Solution

After you've dialed up the pain, it's time to show the audience *your* solution. This may be your product or service, your diagnostic process, an appointment with you or exam by you, or otherwise engaging with you. I've made this fifth in the sequence. If you get to it too quickly, you have not laid groundwork needed for your solution to be readily accepted. If you get to it too late, you may frustrate your audience. There is a sweet spot in the sequence for this, and we're confident from experience with literally thousands of presentations that this is it: fifth.

A big mistake that a lot of people make with presentations is to move from stating the solution to teaching the solution. Unless you are a school teacher, with kids in a classroom, you do *not* want to actually teach. I guess I'm a salesman by instinct or impulse, so this was not hard for me to understand and

CHAPTER 5 / THE SPEAKER'S FORMULA™

accept, but Dustin is a technical thinker, so his temptation is always to explain how and why something works as it does and exactly how to use it. He and I watch many people struggle with this. Decide on *the* purpose of your presentation: to influence or persuade, to make an immediate sale, or to set in motion a selling process. Decide on *the action* you want from the audience. Everything in the presentation is to serve this purpose, and anything that doesn't gets left, as they say in Hollywood, on the cutting room floor. Real teaching almost always goes six steps too far and raises as many doubts and questions as it answers. You want people to know you have a solution and to be excited about it without getting bogged down in its details.

## 6: Set Expectations

An audience needs to know where they are going with you. They don't want to board an airplane, embark on a cruise, or join you in your presentation without a good idea of the destination and the landmark points along the way. Any uncertainty raises anxiety. So, you need to tell them what you are going to tell them.

Also on a more sophisticated level, you want to try to direct and control their reactions to your presentation. This is sometimes called framing or pre-framing. By setting these expectations, you create an *open loop* in their minds, particularly in their subconscious minds. How they feel about and respond to what you say, do, and ask of them during the rest of your presentation will loop back to what you told them to expect.

I often use a very simple, four-point "rap" in my presentations that goes something like this:

*I've got three rules before we begin . . . Rule #1: We're going to have fun. Is it OK with everybody if we have fun? Good. Rule*

*#2: I promise to give you 110%. Is it OK with everybody if I give you 110%? Good. Rule #3: This is going to be an interactive presentation. The more you give to me, the more feedback I get, the more I give to you. Is that fair? Great. Then the bonus Rule #4 is: You'll take action. You won't just listen and leave. You'll decide and do. You know success comes down to taking action, right? Great . . .*

This creates a "yes energy" with the audience. When the time comes for them to make a (buying) decision and take an action, they have been pre-framed to do it and have even agreed in advance to do it.

## 7: Social Proof

When you present a product, service, or just an idea, people have objections and doubts. Most buyers start out as nonbuyers. Most believers start out as skeptics. Maybe, in their mind, they're saying, "I don't have time," or, "it won't work for me." They're saying *something,* and it will likely be a reason not to go forward. The antidote is *targeted* social proof. When we build a presentation for and with a Speaking Empire client, we typically identify 5 to 7 typical objections or doubts likely held by large percentages of their audiences. Then we find 5 to 7 matching social proof stories, testimonials, or fact-filled case histories. Each erases one of the 5, 6, or 7.

## 8: Show Benefits

This is elementary, but it still needs to be said: People do not buy a product to have the product or even because of its features. They don't even buy the benefits of the product. They buy the benefits of the benefits. Nobody buys fast-drying paint because it dries fast, or even because of the benefit of that: less chances of it being touched, smudged, dirt falling onto it. They're buying *time* and *freedom* (from drudgery). Virtually every presentation needs at least one slide that lists or depicts the benefits of the benefits.

## 9: Irresistible Offer

Think about offers as "1 to 10." 1 is basic, ordinary, and/or unexciting. 10 is absolutely overpowering, "must have," urgent, and exciting. Think about the offer you are going to make with your presentation. Is it a 1, a 3, a 5, a 7? It is hard to get to 10—to absolutely irresistible—but the closer you get, the better. A great presentation can fall flat and fail if it brings everybody to an unexciting offer.

Usually, you will build value by listing and describing every separate item of the product or service, or even of something like a private appointment, call, or exam. For health-care practices, Dan Kennedy invented the "5 Questions That Will Be Answered at Your Exam" and "What To Expect at Your First Appointment" lists back in the 1980s and has kept these in health-care practice and financial services marketing to this day.

There's a lot more about this in Dustin's Chapter 6 on Irresistible Offer Architecture®.

## 10: No-Risk Guarantee

The number-one reason people do not respond to the offer you make with your presentation is that they feel they were let down *by somebody else*. As you are presenting, they are remembering! A strong, simple, straightforward guarantee gives them needed reassurance that they can make a decision with you without getting burned.

You might ask: How long should a guarantee be? I've done extensive testing of this myself. In over 3,000 presentations for my own products and services, I've offered 7-day, 30-day, 6-month, and 12-month guarantees. Which do you think converted the best?

Most guess 12 months. Actually, there's very little difference between 7 days, 12 months, and anything in between. What matters is that you have an appropriate guarantee. If they can judge in 7 days, then that's fine. If they need a month, then a month. What's most important is that you have a guarantee, period. (See Figure 5.2.)

### 11: Give Deadline

In Point 9 on page 36, I talked about how you build value as part of an Irresistible Offer. You create urgency to act immediately with

**FIGURE 5.2:** Guarantee

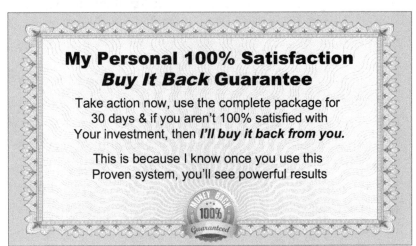

a deadline and with fast-action bonuses. People procrastinate. It's what they do.

The last thing you want is a presentation that lets the audience off the hook and lets them meander out of the room or exit your webinar to think things over. The whole point of doing powerful group presentations is efficiency. The last thing you want to wind up doing is chasing people who saw your presentation, by email, mail, or phone. My goal is to have a presentation that will have people dancing and running—not walking—to the back of the room to buy or sign up for whatever next step is offered.

A lot of people will do this with now-or-never discounts. This can be effective, but I personally never like lowering prices because it's what everybody does. Other techniques are fast-action bonuses, a limited bonus only for the first x-number, or an impending event, like a fast-start class, breakfast, lunch, or online session within hours or the very next day. In any case, the deadline itself must be very clear. If for some reason, it is not immediate and it is within, say, 90 minutes after the webinar, consider displaying a countdown clock by the order page and sending at least one email going out: "Just 29 minutes left."

## 12: Call to Action

I see so many people who seem afraid to make the call to action and tell people exactly what to do and to do it now. You need to be very direct about this. You can tell them to get up and go to the table at the back to schedule an appointment or quickly complete a form and buy the product. You can have forms handed out as you are getting to this point in your presentation and tell them to fill them out and take them to back tables, "the folks in the red jackets at the doors," or to bring them up to the front to you. If you are delivering your presentation in a physical location, it's a bad idea to be sending them to some location outside of that room and out of your sight. If you are delivering a presentation online as a webinar or webcast, this step should be easy and seamless. Whatever they are supposed to do as the response to your presentation, they should be told exactly what to do.

I want to emphasize that you can count on this Formula. I have written over 500 presentations for use in 43 different industries and professions, in 109 countries around the world! With a Signature Presentation built with this Formula you really can go ANYWHERE and sell ANYTHING.

---

To download a larger version of the Speaker's Formula™ along with additional valuable presentation creation tools, visit http://NoBSPresentations.com/bonuses.

---

# CHAPTER 6

# Irresistible Offer Architecture®

by Dustin Mathews

ersuading people can be extremely difficult, just difficult, comparatively easy, or very easy. One of the things that moves the needle on that scale is the offer itself. A lot of people do *not* understand this. They worry over every other part of a presentation, particularly the visual elements—slides, graphics, video, stories, and themselves. Ultimately, people buy what they really want and do what they really want to do. When an offer connects with that, it alone can drive extraordinary results from an un-ordinary, just serviceable presentation.

When you have an irresistible offer advantage, you can:

- Sell without having to hard sell;

- Sell at a premium price instead of a price like competitors' or at discounts;
- Attract new clients, patients, or customers easily.

I created what we now use at Speaking Empire for just about every presentation we build, our Irresistible Offer Architecture®, out of a need to have a blueprint that would enable any speaker or presenter to offer any product or service to any audience anywhere, by any media, and get a desirable result. Further, I wanted it to be "fill in the blank" quick, because, frankly, a lot of people find themselves getting opportunities to speak and giving presentations without the time or without taking time to properly prepare. This blueprint or template allows you to put an offer together on the fly. I confess, I've done it myself.

There are nine keys to Irresistible Offer Architecture®, which I've organized into three triangles shown in Figure 6.1 on page 43.

## Triangle 1: Hot Buttons

Different people have different Hot Buttons (see Figure 6.2, page 44). A Hot Button is the one that, when pushed, sets off the strongest possible "I want that—and I want it now—regardless of what I have to do or pay" response. Think about yourself: You do have at least one if not several such buttons, just as you have a Hot Button that triggers your temper, a Hot Button that triggers sexual arousal, and so on. This is why the Audience Knowledge that Dan Kennedy described in Chapter 3 and the benefits of benefits secret that Dave revealed in Chapter 5 are so important.

Let's assume you have a product or service that is just not connecting with the Hot Buttons of your audience members and you can't figure out why. I always challenge myself with

**FIGURE 6.1:** The Nine Keys to Irresistible Offer Architecture®

this: I suppose that no one in my audience will be Hot-Button motivated by any part of my product, service, or offer. Maybe I'm doing a presentation about cancer, offering colonoscopy exams, or I'm a CPA offering a second-opinion review of your last three years' tax returns. They have benefits and benefits of benefits, but still, they aren't exciting. I will turn to the bonus. One of the most famous examples of this, from TV commercials—which *are* presentations—comes from *Sports Illustrated* magazine. A great presentation about *Sports Illustrated* might sell an acceptable number of subscriptions, but offering the "football phone" (yes,

**FIGURE 6.2:** Triangle 1: Hot Buttons

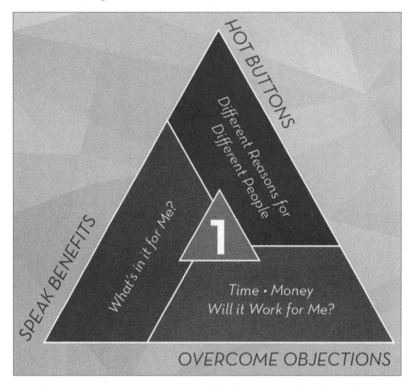

before smartphones, in the days of landlines) sold an amazing number of subscriptions. People who didn't really care about the magazine couldn't resist the football-shaped phone. Keywords: couldn't resist. This ties to Triangle 2.

## Triangle 2: Added Value

Everything has *intrinsic* value. Here is the dictionary definition of intrinsic:

intrinsic
*adjective*

belonging naturally; essential: *access to the arts is **intrinsic** to a high quality of life.*

• (of a muscle) contained wholly within the organ on which it acts.

DERIVATIVES

**intrinsically** adverb

ORIGIN late 15th cent. (in the general sense [interior, inner]): from French **intrinsèque**, from late Latin **intrinsecus**, from the earlier adverb **intrinsecus** *"inwardly, inward."*

**Thesaurus**

intrinsic

*an intrinsic eye for fashion,* inherent, innate, inborn, inbred, congenital, connate, natural; deep-rooted, deep-seated, indelible, ineradicable, ingrained; integral, basic, fundamental, essential; built-in.

In other words—it's about what something is.

But a truly powerful presentation of any product or service focuses on personal and emotional reasons to have it. Its value is made by those things. For example, we know that scarcity or assumed or perceived scarcity causes people to make buying decisions faster and to pay more than they would if buying in a calmer environment. Go to an auction and watch this happen all around you. You'll even hear bidding stall, often at a right price, then start up again in a renewed frenzy when just one person surrenders to pressure and bids a new, higher number.

Marketers talk about price-value equations (see Figure 6.3 on page 46). You could picture a two-sided scale, with price

**FIGURE 6.3:** Triangle 2: Added Value

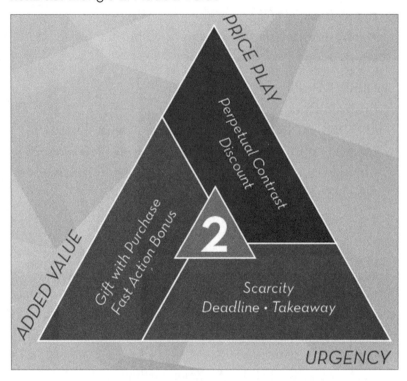

on one side and value on the other. When value feels like it is much, much higher than price, people in an audience surrender to an irresistible price-value equation. They literally sat there watching, saying to themselves, "No, I'm not going to buy this. No, I'm still not going to buy this. No, I'm s-t-i-l-l n-o-t going to buy this. Oh, OK, gee, how could I *not* buy this?"

There are two ways to get this effect.

The obvious one is deep discounting against a real or artificially inflated price. The trouble with this is that it can cost you serious money or, if artificial, it can compromise your credibility. Some presenters also feel badly about the tactic, and any negative feelings you hold about what you are doing *will* be smelled by an audience. You can use this, but use it cautiously.

The other one I like better is Perpetual Contrast. For example, my real estate training course is $1,000.00 but it will help you become a real estate millionaire in 36 months or less, and it is as complete and systematic as a McDonald's® franchise that would cost you $250,000.00. The contrast is $1,000.00 vs. $1 million, and $1,000.00 vs. $250,000.00. You can also contrast to trivial items: That same $1,000.00 system making you a millionaire in three years costs you just 91 cents a day, and you can't make a Starbucks stop once a day for that.

For a presentation used by orthodontists providing top-level treatment at premium fees, Dan Kennedy used references to other purchase decisions that affluent and discerning people make when they choose to buy higher quality, higher priced goods or services than they have to—home furnishings, automobiles, vacation travel and accommodations. These are compared to and contrasted with $7,000.00 to $9,000.00 Invisalign® braces and treatment, which has the added benefit of gently shaming the parent who thinks that $7,000.00 is a lot to pay for their kid's braces, when they spend that much flying first class and staying at a top resort for a few days, when coach and cheaper hotels were options.

In our field, with seminars, we can often make a case tied to nominal income increase. If, for example, a seminar carries a price tag of $5,000.00, and you earn—or intend to earn—$200,000.00 a year, the fee is only a measly 2.5%. We say: Do you really think you can go through this entire seminar and not go home empowered to increase your income by at least 2.5%?

### Triangle 3: Reassurance

Dave said that the number-one reason why somebody in your audience doesn't accept your offer is that they remember a time or times when they believed somebody like you about some comparable promises and feel they were let down or deceived. This can explain why 100 people go to the trouble of coming to watch your presentation as a webinar, and stay all the way to the end, but only 20 purchase your product.

People can get reassurance several different ways. See Figure 6.4.

One is by your guarantee or guarantees, which Dave discussed.

**FIGURE 6.4:** Triangle 3: Reassurance

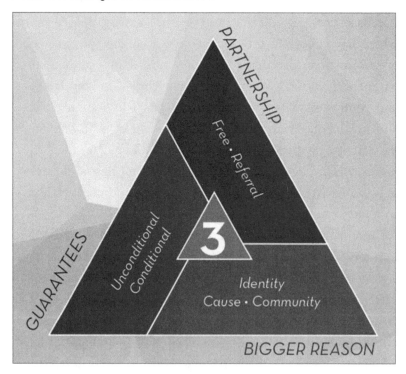

Another is a *bigger reason* they identify with. An example is the business donating a percentage of sales to a charity or worthy cause the audience has affinity for—like The Wounded Warrior Project, to which boomers and seniors have affinity, or as Dan Kennedy does, to animal and animal rescue charities. Or if the business has a mission, or a movement—as Trump characterized his campaign, so people are supporting and are part of something bigger and more important than just the transaction. This can provide a good story, halo-effect credibility, pictures, and video for your presentations.

Another way people get reassurance is by identifying with a *bigger* reason (for doing business with you). This works so well it is illegal in certain fields. In the seminar world where Dave and I do a lot of work, it is not uncommon for the seminar promoter to let certain people attend an event free if they get two or three of their "tribe" to pay the fee to attend. The technicalities of this are beyond this book, but know it is a possibility. An audience can be motivated by some secondary opportunity they must first own and use the offered product or service to get.

As shown in Figure 6.5 on page 50, these Triangles connect with each other, and when you can use all three, you make it very hard for people to say no to your offer, which *is* the goal!

**FIGURE 6.5:** Irresistible Offer Architecture® Blueprint

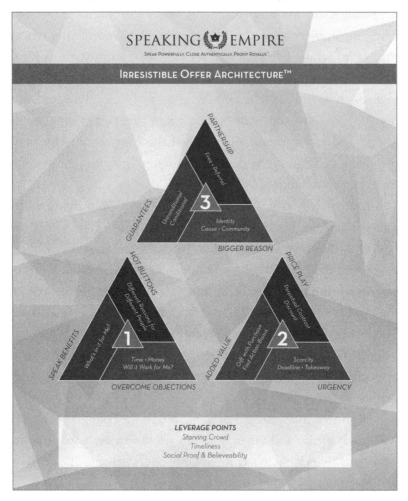

To download a larger copy of this Irresistible Offer Architecture®
Three-Triangle illustration along with real world examples of its
application in different kinds of businesses, go to:
http://NoBSPresentations.com/bonus offer.

To see an Irresistible Offer created out of thin air before
a live audience, watch the amazing video at:
http://NoBSPresentations.com/bonuses.

CHAPTER 7

# The Structure of Promises

by Dan Kennedy

The Irresistible Offer—the one those in your audience would crawl across broken glass on naked knees to get—is the heart and soul of a great presentation. Creating and delivering anything less is a squandering of some of the opportunity you obtained by being able to make a presentation, and squandering opportunity is a sin!

One way to think about your Irresistible Offer is as the means of fulfilling a magnificent, desired promise. Great presentations make great promises.

My famous Magnetic Marketing System® presentation, responsible for selling tens of millions of dollars of that System and bringing tens of thousands of customers into my businesses, was usually delivered to audiences comprised of independent, small-business owners and sales professionals. Very early in it, I made each group an irresistible promise . . .

> *If you are a small-business owner, you are an advertising victim. After today, you will never again spend even one dollar on advertising without knowing it directly brings you customers, sales, and profits.*

> *If you are a sales professional, after today, you will never again need to do "cold" prospecting.*

Later, my Irresistible Offer provided the means—in this case the take-home tool kit—of fulfilling those promises.

## Four Ways to Structure a Great Promise

There are different kinds of promises and structures for promises. Most people do put them into presentations, but most people put in weak and poorly designed ones. Here are the four ways to structure a great promise.

### #1: BIG Stated Promises versus Small, Implied Promises

Examples of ordinary, small promises are:

1. Learn how to boost your immune system
2. 50 tips for a more bountiful garden
3. The five best hiding places in your home for your valuables
4. Amazing home remedies that heal without drugs or doctors
5. There is a new frontier in America—making some who are "in the know" rich

All five of these have two flaws in common. First, they share implication. The direct, personal benefit to you is not boldly stated, but left for you to get for yourself from the statement. Second, they are small and rather timid. They're all "good," but not "great."

Here they are, re-crafted as big, stated promises:

#1

DISCOVER THE SECRETS OF PEOPLE WHO NEVER GET SICK!

#2

GET 50 TIPS FROM MASTER GARDENERS AND GROW TWICE THE GARDEN FOR HALF THE COST—AND MAKE YOUR NEIGHBORS GREEN WITH ENVY!

#3

FOIL EVEN PROFESSIONAL BURGLARS AND THIEVES SO THEY CAN NEVER FIND YOUR VALUABLES HIDDEN IN YOUR OWN HOME.

#4

LIVE AT LEAST 15 YEARS LONGER THAN YOUR "LIFE EXPECTANCY"—AND STAY OUT OF THE HOSPITAL, AND RARELY NEED A DOCTOR, EVEN STAY OFF OF PRESCRIPTION DRUGS!

#5

YOU CAN GET VERY RICH, VERY FAST—IF YOU'LL JOIN THOSE "IN THE KNOW" ABOUT "THE NEW FRONTIER" IN AMERICA.

You can see that the stated, big-promise rewrites lend themselves much better to Irresistible Offers.

## #2: *Promises Framed as Questions*

In some situations, for various reasons, you may not want to make a direct, stated, big promise. In these cases, you can frame the promise as a question or even a series of questions, still setting up an Irresistible Offer. Here are several actual examples from different presentations:

### A

YOU—A Millionaire? Did you know there's a new millionaire explosion going on in America right now? More ordinary men and women rose to the ranks of millionaires this year than any prior year. How can this be? Do they share a secret? If you knew their secret, could you and would you be willing to follow simple 1–2–3, A–B–C directions, and invest as little as one hour a day?

### B

Have you ever noticed there seem to be some people who can eat whatever they want, as much as they want—but never gain weight? What if everything you've been told about dieting is wrong? If you could actually reset your metabolism to burn more body fat without starving or exercising, would you be . . . ?

### C

If you could be guaranteed financial gains but fully protected against losses, if you could share in the upside of a rising stock market but never risk more than 20% of your principal, would you want to know about this special investment strategy? What if you could be "in the market" but never again have a worried, sleepless night? Is it possible to double your retirement income without any risk?

The beauty of these questions in presentations is that people hear the promises and don't really hear the question marks punctuating them. The promise is what "sticks," so you can loop back to it with your Irresistible Offer.

### #3: *Primary Promises and Secondary Promises*

You more than double the impact of a primary promise by following it with several reinforcing, secondary promises. As an example, for my Magnetic Marketing System®, for salespeople, my primary promise is: put an end to "cold" prospecting once and for all. That produces a number of secondary benefits that can also be promised:

- Now you can invest 100% of your time in actually selling—not hunting for someone to sell to.
- You can double or triple your income easily and automatically, when you're able to stop wasting time on prospecting.
- You'll be the envy of everybody else in the office—when they watch good, quality prospects literally line up to talk to you, without you ever making a cold call or suffering through another networking event to get them.
- With the stress of never quite knowing where your next prospect is coming from—or when—erased, you can relax and enjoy selling again.
- You'll be home on time for dinner! Your spouse, kids, and friends will notice the difference in you.

A good rule of thumb is three to five secondary promises for each primary promise.

If you prefer, these three can all be reframed as questions, per #4. Either way, again, your Irresistible Offer loops back to them.

### #4: Complex, Stacked Promises

Dale Carnegie's and Napoleon Hill's famous bestselling books' titles delivered two-part, stacked promises:

(1) Win Friends and (2) Influence People

(1) Grow Rich with (2) Peace of Mind

Arguably, either one would be a good enough promise, but stacked the sum has more impact than $1 + 1 = 2$.

A promise for my training is complex. It stacks three promises:

You get a (1) Marketing Message that is magnetically attractive plus (2) the ability to target the right Market certain to be responsive plus (3) the ability to choose and use the best Media to deliver your Message to the Market.

A very successful presentation for a luxury time-share vacation club stacked its promises this way:

(1) You stay in magnificent, multi-million-dollar mansions, lakefront and beachfront homes, and ski and golf resort homes—never hotels or condos, with (2) complete privacy, (3) made ready for your stay to your liking, by your instructions, (4) all-inclusive, with no hidden or surprise charges and (5) your satisfaction completely guaranteed.

Such complex promises might not be practical in advertising given impatient and fleeting attention, but in a presentation delivered to a captive audience in a physical location, or to a deliberately tuned-in audience at a webcast or online video, a multi-item, stacked promise can work well. It can be repeated. It can be said and shown on slide or screen graphically. It can be dissected and re-assembled. When looped back to the Irresistible Offer, there's a higher level of support for the offer than by any single, simple promise.

Once you decide on and craft your presentation's promise or promises, and decide on the Irresistible Offer that fulfills or facilitates fulfillment of the promises, you have the foundation of and the bookends for your presentation. In a sense, everything between the promise and the fulfillment by Irresistible Offer is a bridge the audience is guided across. You are literally leading them to The Promised Land!

# CHAPTER 8

# Presentainer® Secrets of Mass Persuasion

by Dave VanHoose

There's not much real certainty in business or in life.

I've been involved in selling by presentations for a very long time, and I believe I *know* a number of things about it, but I am also always still learning and, hopefully, improving. I was asked at a seminar if I could talk about any one thing about creating and delivering presentations that was a rock-solid certainty. There is.

The more experience I got with developing presentations and with delivering them as a speaker, the more certain I became that . . .

**The more you teach,**

**the less you sell.**

In the beginning, I fell into the trap that catches most speakers and presenters: being a professor. I learned that it is much more useful to be a Presentainer®—our word at Speaking Empire for somebody who can move an audience emotionally, connect with them personally, and entertain them on some level. This is the only way to hold attention and grow interest. It makes you more memorable and your presentation more influential. It involves the audience as they like to be involved. The TV they watch, the movies they see twice, the games they play, and the novels they read all do this, and so should you.

Here's what being a Presentainer® looks like:

Figure 8.1 shows that if you have a powerful presentation, as we've been discussing, *and* you have the right mindset about it, yourself, and your audience, *and* you have the right delivery, you win every time. Let's talk about delivery.

**FIGURE 8.1:** Presentation/Delivery/Mindset Triangle

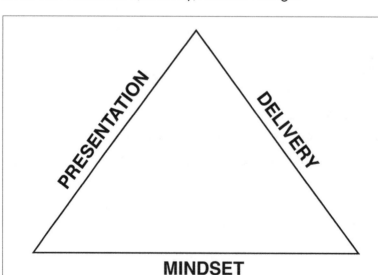

## 1: Leading and Ending

The classic, textbook speaking formula applies: tell them what you are going to tell them, tell them, then tell them what you told them. This lets you first create a sense of anticipation, getting the audience sitting on the edge of their seats and hanging on every word. Most of the great stage magicians of the golden era, Houdini included, always told the audience about the illusion they would next see, in very dramatic terms—they didn't just go out on stage and perform the trick. At the other end, you summarize what you have told and shown them, because people tend to very quickly forget key points of any complex presentation.

## 2: The Yes State

Small commitments lead to more substantial commitments. Resistance is better erased a little bit at a time. As a presenter, your goal is to have people say yes to you, mentally and physically, a number of times during your presentation. You can involve people by getting them to raise their hands, yell a word or phrase of agreement—"Yes" will do, even getting "all those who . . ." to stand up. With most audiences, there is limited response to the first attempt at this, and you have to joke with them and cajole them to get more of them to play.

At Speaking Empire, we usually build some Yes State questions, requests for agreement, and moments into every presentation.

A lot of things can affect the audience's state: who they are, how they came into the audience—willingly or "sent" by an employer—time of day and fatigue, what they know in advance about you and your presentation, and location. This hands you two responsibilities: first, to do what you can to help get them into a positive mental attitude about you and your presentation's benefits and benefits of benefits before they are actually with you. Second, to be able to "take the temperature" of a group and make some adjustments on the fly if it is cold, to warm it up. The first of these is really all about marketing, and I suggest reading Dan Kennedy's book *No B.S. Guide to Trust-Based Marketing* for a lot of good guidance.

The one thing *never* to do is to leave an audience's mental and emotional state to random chance and try to deal with it in a single leap over a tall wall toward the end of your presentation.

## 3: The Seven-Minute Rule

Have you ever seen a speaker start strong but lose his audience sometime during his presentation? The audience starts slumping, fidgeting, and even looking at their phones—at worst, getting up and leaving—one after another. In making Speaking Empire the go-to company for developing powerful presentations, we've done a lot of research, as well as drawn from our own experience. One of the areas where there is a lot of research to be had is in the neurosciences. One fact for which there is consensus is that the human brain can only maintain focus for seven minutes. It basically fades, stops, and restarts in seven-minute cycles. That's why you need to get your audience to re-engage with you every seven minutes. You can do this with a quick request or direction, like:

- Raise your hand if _____
- You'll want to write *this* down.
- Stand up if—or—stand up and do _____

- Turn to your neighbor and _____
- Repeat after me . . .

## 4: Dynamism

Few effective speakers stand still behind a podium or lectern, or read a word-for-word speech from notes or a teleprompter. It doesn't have enough life to it. Audiences are affected as much or more by how you say what you say as they are by what you are saying. That "how" includes voice, confidence, enthusiasm, whether or not you seem to be happy to be in front of them delivering your message, and physical movement. In many ways, you are a performer delivering a performance.

> To learn more about being a Presentainer®, visit www.SpeakingEmpire.com/presentainer.

CHAPTER 9

# Demonstration in Presentations

by Dan Kennedy

*S*eeing is believing. It's one of the oldest clichés, for good reason.

As one of my hobbies, I'm a student of the history of the art of deception, and one of the areas of life and commerce where it has been practiced most ardently, artfully, and consistently is with psychic phenomena. From simple ouiji board, tarot card, and crystal ball readings to psychics claiming to contact and channel communication from the dead to the living, people are made to believe, and believers are defrauded of their money and dignity by con artists who have mastered convincing *physical* demonstrations of their psychic abilities. The book *The Heyday of Spiritualism* published in 1970 is one of hundreds of exposé and how-to books chronicling the popularity of mediums, psychics, faith healers, and the like, from the earliest days of the 1900s. Despite all the education and information that has become available since then, the exact same tricks used then are used now by scammers plying these trades. The only difference now is that some of them get their own reality TV shows.

For the record, it is *all* charlatanism, deception, and fraud— often cruel.

I mention it as **a demonstration of the power of demonstration** for presenters. The séance was and still is the number-one type of demonstration-presentation of this industry. People gather in a room that must go dark, as a medium supposedly rendered unable to move by hands held and feet bound or locked in a cabinet or some other means connects with The Other Side, and a ghostly presence speaks through her but also lifts the table, knocks objects off shelves, ruffles one of the attendees' hair, empties a glass of water. The medium may also emit ectoplasm from her private parts, speak in tongues, vibrate, and collapse. Another favored demonstration is the "cold read," where the psychic tells people things about themselves he couldn't possibly know, often in concert with aid from each person's dearly departed, and conveys heartfelt messages from the dead parents or children. When it is done well, it's hard to disbelieve what you are seeing.

Faith healing is of the same school of trickery. People still, to this day, leave America, travel to distant third-world countries, and hand over large sums to "miracle workers" who can deliver incredibly convincing demonstrations of opening a person's body with no knife or scalpel—just bare hands or even mind power—and withdrawing blackened lumps of cancer or evil spirit manifestations, curing the afflicted and desperate people, although the demonstrations to the customer or the audience of prospective customers is usually done with a professional performer and co-conspirator pretending to be riddled with a disease and near death. It's all bunk. But when it is done well, it's hard to disbelieve what you are seeing.

Houdini did his level best to debunk many of these fraudsters, yet Arthur Conan Doyle famously believed Houdini's harsh criticism of the psychics and spiritualists was just a cover-up, as was his magic; Doyle believed Houdini himself actually had magical and psychic powers!

*This is what physical demonstration does. It creates, magnifies, and solidifies belief because an audience believes what it sees. When it is done well, it's hard to disbelieve what you are seeing.*

In selling, one-to-one, in the home, in offices and clinics, and to groups, physical demonstration has long played a chief role, and many of these demonstrations have not gone away either. The incredible blender/food processor is still demonstrated today on TV, in stores, and at food and home and garden shows exactly as it was demonstrated 20 years ago, 30, 40, 50 years ago. The same Tupperware® demonstration first devised by Brownie Wise in the 1950s is still used by Tupperware's party plan agents in living rooms all around the world today. I learned and used demonstrations like that for a number of products in my earliest years, selling to people in their homes. I later devised demonstrations for use in TV infomercials. I have a whale of a lot of experience with demonstration, and I assure you regardless of who you are, what you sell, where or how you sell it, whatever presentation to develop and deliver will be multiplied in power if a compelling seeing-is-believing demonstration can be added.

You may think there is no way to demonstrate what you sell or do in a demonstration to an audience—and you are almost certainly wrong. Figuring out demonstrations for tangible products is relatively easy. The aforementioned magic blender into which you can stick a whole watermelon and get juice, the knife that cuts a tomato into paper thin slices right after being used to carve wood or cut a metal nail in half, the red copper pan nothing will stick to, the amazing car polish so protective you pour gas all over the hood, light it, extinguish it, and there's not even a smoke smudge. But you can demonstrate the intangible as well.

If you've ever been to a network marketing company "opportunity meeting," you know about "The Circles." For a tiny group in a living room or on stage in front of hundreds or even thousands, somebody draws the circles on the whiteboard: You only have to bring six people into the business, then they each get six, then they each get six, etc., etc., and you are atop a gigantic, mushrooming constellation of busy-bee distributors from which money is passing upstream to you. But it is one thing seeing red and blue and green circles drawn on a whiteboard. It was a very different thing the Saturday I watched an Amway leader by the name of Charlie Marsh get 20 helpers on stage to unroll a huge, seven-foot-high and as wide as the room roll of brown butcher paper on which photos of everybody in his organization through its first eight levels had been glued on in the same pattern as you would draw the circles, with lines connecting them, and he walked around in front pointing to different ones he could tell the audience about but also admitting he'd never even met most of them, and then pointing to six at the top connected directly to him and saying, "They're the only ones I recruited." *That* was a demonstration!

In my speech that sold tens of millions of dollars of my home study course and tool kit for small-business owners called *The Magnetic Marketing System®,* I built in demonstration. All the promised results were intangible. There was no physical way to show customers of a business receiving direct-mail sequences, reading, then coming into businesses because of the System. The product itself was paper pages in a notebook—remarkably unexciting. But I could do a show-and-tell demonstration. The now famous series of Giorgio letters for the Italian restaurant owner turned Romance Director can be seen in my book *The Ultimate Sales Letter, 4th Edition.* I explained these, showed them on the big screen as I read portions of them, emphasized what they demonstrated as I went, and ended with the flourish of a rhetorical question: *Do you honestly believe that anybody receiving these four letters does not know all about Giorgio's, isn't showing the letters to their spouse, neighbors, and friends? For four postage stamps, we've made him famous almost overnight in his market!*

That "bit" in my presentation became so well-known and loved, that audiences asked me to do it again and again as they became part of my permanent audience attending seminars over years.

For some years, I had a client who was the reigning authority on stopping employee and deliveryman theft in the supermarket and convenience store industry, and he delivered presentations to that industry's company owners, executives, and store managers about 100 times a year. Most were skeptical of his information, believing their chief problems were with shoplifters. We devised a dramatic demonstration. He brought a "denier" manager up on stage, set up a fake delivery in a fake store, and challenged the manager to block every attempt to steal from him as the bread deliveryman—then right in front of everybody—robbed the poor victim blind. For another client who sells incoming call training to dentists, we devised a secret shopping and recording of the actual offices of the doctors who will be in an audience at a convention, then he plays the recordings of their own staffs' bungling of calls from the stage for all to hear, one after the other, until the group yells, "We surrender!" For a financial advisor specializing in reducing tax bites into retirees' 401(k) and IRA payouts, at his free seminars for seniors, I have him bring several folks up to the front of the room, giving them each a real $100.00 bill and a cigarette lighter and instructing them to burn the money just like they are with their poor tax strategies. Many can't bring themselves to do it. Their hands shake. When he then puts about 20 of the $100.00 bills in a metal tray—representing the average losses of a retiree from his IRA payouts to unnecessary taxes—and pours lighter fluid all over it, the audience erupts and begs him not to burn the pile of money. When they have all agreed they shouldn't either, he sets aside the lighter fluid and promises to donate the $2,000.00 instead to a charity named by one of the people in the front row.

There is a demonstration, and often a dramatic, high-impact, and memorable demonstration, to be created for every intangible service or product. If you don't create and use one, you are depriving yourself of one of the key elements of the most powerful presentation possible.

> For more about this, and about Dan's life in selling by speaking, and all his methods, get a copy of his book *Speak to Sell*.

CHAPTER 10

# Someone To Speak and
## Present To

by Dustin Mathews

While this is a book all about the maximum-effectiveness presentation itself, there's no point to it without an audience for it!

With that in mind, I'm going to talk a little bit about the live event and the assembly of the audience.

I've made my living from doing a lot of live events in physical locations with audiences. There are many benefits to this. First of all, creating an event and offering it to a target market or the public immediately gives you some level of celebrity status and can position you as an expert. After all, when is there an *event* promoted and held starring a nobody?

Live events are a staple of the entertainment industry. Movie stars aren't just seen in movies, but at live events—

movie premieres, red carpets at award events, the Cannes Film Festival, Comic-Con. These are breathlessly reported on by the media and eagerly watched by millions of people. Athletes' games are live events. In this past presidential election, Donald Trump lived by the live event attended by thousands, much grander in theater and spectacle than most political gatherings. Even a small live event can wrap you in status, importance, and celebrity. For many years, a client of Dan Kennedy's, a genealogy researcher, did a speaking tour once a year, conducting small group presentations at public libraries and bookstores, typically drawing only 15 or 20 to each event. But to them, she was a Very Important Expert, by virtue of the library or bookstore having promoted her event. From these, she secured all the individual clients she could handle, for whom she did comprehensive family history research projects, at fees from $5,000.00 to $25,000.00 each.

The live event can also be a great place to show off existing clients to new, prospective clients. Smart cosmetic surgeons or dentists who hold live events for potential patients always have at least several of their proudest, happiest, most beautiful patients there to be introduced, interviewed, met, and mingled with.

Your own live event is the perfect place to deliver your own presentation, because there is no interference from others, no limitations or rules to adhere to, and the assembled audience has come to see and hear from you.

As you know, Dan, Dave, and I are big believers in one-to-many selling. It's worth a fair amount of money and effort to get a group of 50 prospects together in one place at one time, weighed against the time cost of meeting with 50 different people individually and delivering the presentation one-to-one 50 times.

*There are a few different kinds of live events you might want to use.*

One is commonly called the "preview seminar." You may be familiar with the real estate investing industry's version of these, typically promoted on radio, on TV, in newspapers, and by mail as well as online, and held in hotels—often once in an afternoon and again that evening at five different locations in a circle around a city, five days in a row. Like these, most preview seminars are typically brief—from 90 minutes to 2 hours—so they can be done as lunch-and-learn events or held as evening seminars. They are introductory in nature, sometimes leading to registration for a subsequent multiday seminar, to follow-up appointments, or both.

A very successful financial advisor in Michigan conducts two-hour preview seminars at community colleges, libraries, and community centers about maximizing Social Security, Medicare, and other government benefits for retirees. At these, he moves people to a full day, 9:00 A.M. to 5:00 P.M. seminar on safe retirement investing. Five or six of the preview seminars feed into one of the full-day seminars, usually held on a Saturday. Out of that daylong seminar, individual appointments are set with interested, qualified potential clients to whom customized financial plans, annuities, insurance, and precious metals investments can be sold.

Another is the "customer appreciation event." This may be a seminar or workshop or a less formal social gathering. In either case, past and present customers are encouraged to attend with family, friends, and co-workers. Pastors rent movie theaters, show a family-friendly movie, and invite parishioners and their friends to attend. Usually, the pastor makes only a few welcoming remarks—there is no presentation, but he's there to greet and meet, there's church literature, and some promotion for an upcoming event at the church takes place. Others using this exact same movie theater/film night event include martial arts academy owners, orthodontists, and financial advisors. A customer appreciation event more suitable to an introductory presentation is a lunch or dinner with a guest speaker or celebrity in addition to yourself, possibly a local sports or TV celebrity.

Finally, there is the "real" seminar or boot camp. These are at least one day in length but usually two to four days. This is a great venue to sell high-end, complex "programs," services, or bundles of products and services. You have the luxury of time, a choreographed build-up to the sales presentation and multiple opportunities to support the sale before and after the presentation. Attendees can be badged or otherwise identified as being owners of or participants in the program being sold. They can be brought up on stage to be interviewed about their successful experiences and/or given awards. The entire event can be organized to support the one thing being sold and its sales presentation, or time can be apportioned so that multiple products or services can each get their own presentations.

*Whatever kind of event you decide to do, you'll have to choose a place, date, and time.*

If you are holding a local event for people in your city or a chosen city, be sure to take traffic and traffic patterns and other local events, into consideration. Dave and I once neglected checking on community events and had an Ironman Triathlon taking place, blocking off three of the four streets around the hotel we were holding a preview seminar in. In some cities, typically those designed as spokes-and-wheel, a central location can be best. In others, where there is great resistance to crossing an east-west or north-south dividing line, you may need to hold your event twice, once on each side of town. Sometimes an airport-adjacent hotel can be easiest to get to by the freeways. If people are flying in to attend, the airport location can be the winner.

If you are holding a bigger event for a national audience and people will be flying in from all over the country, you have to consider seasonal weather, airline hubs and availability of direct flights from other cities, and costs to the travelers. If you want the destination itself to be a magnet, Las Vegas leaps to mind. Everybody likes a good excuse to go to Las Vegas. But you should remember that Vegas is a party city, and there's a lot of competition for the attention and money of your attendees. Dave and I choose not to use Vegas, and I'm fond of Orlando because it's family friendly and readily accessible for the entire country.

*Next, what are the optimal dates for holding your event?*

The answer is: It depends.

If your audience is the general public, for consumer products or services, a weekend might be best as this audience has more flexibility with their schedule than during the week. If your audience is from the corporate world, doing your event on a weekend may not be the smart play because they want to use their time for family, social activities, and recreation. If your audience is from the small-business community, you have to try to find the day or evening that they can be away from their business with the least difficulty. I've found that a lot of chiropractors take Thursdays off but are open on Saturdays, so doing a seminar for them on Thursday might be best. Dan Kennedy had a company for several years that put over 20,000 chiropractors and dentists into preview seminars all over the U.S. and Canada, and he used evenings, 7:00—9:30 P.M., Monday through Thursday.

There are also seasonal considerations. *Monday Night Football* used to make Monday nights during the season impossible. *MNF* has lost some of its exclusivity now, thanks to also having *Sunday* and *Thursday Night Football*, but in most markets with college teams, you can't risk Saturdays.

*Next, what are the optimal times?*

This depends on your audience and market and can be affected by your own logistics. If you are only doing occasional events locally for your business or practice, you can settle on an ideal time. When we were in the business of promoting public preview seminars about real estate investing and were traveling from city to city to do it, we chose to do two previews a day in each place even if that wasn't ideal. It usually cost the same to rent the hotel meeting room for a half or whole day, our travel cost was the same, and our promotion costs were the same, so we settled for smaller audiences at each time to get to a bigger total audience for the entire day than we could achieve with one time. We were young. We experimented a lot, too, and if you are going to do a lot of events, you should too. For example, we tested scheduling our two-hour preview during people's lunch hours from noon to 2:00 P.M. We found that fewer people attended than at any other time, but we had a much higher conversion rate; a higher percentage of the audience enrolled in the program presented. My theory is that the people who had enough flexibility and control over their workday schedules were more in tune with us and our particular offer.

In multiday boot camp, some very successful event holders like to totally consume the attendees' time with sessions starting at 8:00 A.M. or 9:00 A.M. and going into the evening, to 9:00 or 10:00 P.M. But other equally successful event holders prefer giving the groups evenings off to network and socialize with each other—and rest. If you have high-energy subject matter or are doing intense personal development work, you may be able to keep them up and in sessions until 2:00 A.M. I've certainly seen this, and sometimes wonder if personal growth gurus have a secret competition to see who can keep their audiences up the latest. If you have more technical subject matter, I'd think 9:00 A.M. to 5:00 P.M. might be the limit.

With long hours and multiple days, one of the most important decisions you'll make is when to do your most important presentation that sells the products, services, or programs you assembled the entire event to sell. There are many things to consider in making that decision. Does the audience already have a relationship with you, or are you creating trust from scratch at the event? How difficult is the buying decision, and how expensive (to the audience) is the decision? Will they need to phone home like E.T. or pray on it overnight like a devout Baptist? Are you going to offer a special, early A.M. breakfast, next-day lunch, cocktail reception, or fast-start training for those who buy? Think through the timing and agenda placement of your most important presentation very carefully.

*For many people, there is a question of whether your event should be free or involve paid registration.*

In-office events—like health-care classes put on by chiropractors for patients and patients' guests, a preview seminar about implants put on by dentists, a presentation on Roth IRAs given by the financial planner—are almost always provided free of charge. Many preview seminars held in hotels, locally, or done as nationwide tours are also offered free so as not to put a decision barrier in the way. But make no mistake, just because it's free doesn't mean you don't have to hustle nearly as hard to get people registered as if you were charging, and with free events, you may get a bigger number registered, but you'll find many won't honor their commitment, leaving you with empty chairs. A strong post-registration follow-up campaign is almost always needed.

Some events are offered with seat deposits. This is when the people register with their credit cards, with a small seat deposit to guarantee they'll attend, which they forfeit if they don't show up. This can slightly reduce the number registering but as much as double the percentage of those showing up.

In our business, we've moved more and more to paid events, and I like having both an accurate count of what the actual attendance will be and committed, invested attendees. With paid events such as boot camps, we use and recommend using price tiers, like general admission; VIP admission with better reserved seating; and VIP-PLUS, with the best reserved seating and other perks.

*None of this matters if you don't have a way to fill the seats at your events. The most important thing to know about that is: Have many ways, not just one way, if at all possible.*

Ideally, you have your own lists of customers, clients, or patients past, present, and pending who can be invited and urged to bring family, friends, colleagues, or peers. If you are organizing a local event for your local business or practice, you may want to partner with a noncompetitive but compatible business so you can both deliver presentations and each benefit from exposure to the other's lists. Be sure your customers see promotion for your event at every turn, from in-office or in-store signage and fliers to your web and social media sites and ezines.

Whether marketing events locally or nationally, there are relevant trade or professional associations or clubs and organizations who may be persuaded to publicize, support, or even sponsor your events. If you are interested in this, and in lists of such groups, check out the information at http:// NoBSPresentations.com/associations.

Two other good resources are Eventbrite (www.eventbrite. com) and Meetup (www.meetup.com). I like to use them to connect with organizers and make deals. We also love to leverage Meetup at the local level to advertise events. If you need mailing lists to use with direct mail, the big daddy is SRDS (www.SRDS. com), the marketplace of lists to rent. One of my other favorites for list research is at NextMark (https://lists.nextmark.com/ market).

Many people are using Facebook and other social media for events. There is a book in the No B.S. series loaded with information on this, the *No B.S. Guide to Direct-Response Social Media* by Dan Kennedy and Kim Walsh-Phillips. We use paid, targeted Facebook, Google, and YouTube ads for our own events and promote organically through Twitter, LinkedIn, Instagram, and Facebook.

We have clients in financial, investment, and opportunity-related businesses who are still using city newspapers very productively. No, newspapers are not dead, and rates are often reasonable and affordable because a lot of advertisers believe they are dead. Don't ignore the newspaper, especially if your audience age is 55 and older. We have filled a lot of events with the newspaper ad shown in Figure 10.1 on page 82.

**FIGURE 10.1:** Newspaper Ad

Filling seats for events, small or large, is rarely a result of one big, splashy ad campaign or one simple announcement. People are picked off one at a time: one person by a social media post, another by a letter or postcard, another by word of mouth, and so on. Business owners who do a lot of events to promote their

**FIGURE 10.1:** Newspaper Ad, continued

So why am I sharing my secrets? Well a little over three years ago I had just broken my back, was nearly bankrupt, recently divorced and was forced to move in with my dad. I could barely move and the doctor said I couldn't work. But I'm not one for hearing what I can't do. I knew had to find something that I could do that was easy and that could generate some quick cash to cover my piling expenses. So I turned to real estate. And after some trial-and-error, I perfected a very simple system for buying and selling "pre-foreclosure" properties. Keep in mind I had **no experience or formal education.** My friends and I have used this system to create some "extra cash" and free us from our jobs! I've only shared this system with a few of my students and the results have been absolutely amazing!

I've also realized that there are more people in foreclosure than I can possibly help and I really want to assist these people. Let's face it - you can't pick up the newspaper or watch television without seeing the 'flood of foreclosures' that are sweeping the nation. Foreclosures are simply skyrocketing like NO other period in history. Now is the time to get involved!

Never, before have there been as many foreclosures as there are now. Do you remember those commercials claiming that you could buy a half-million dollar house for only $1000 a month!? Banks were handing out mortgages left and right – without even checking credit or income. I bet you can remember thinking "How can they do this?"

It happened…a lot, but now these mortgages are just starting to adjust, creating **unseen amounts of foreclosures,** while causing incredible opportunities across the nation! I wish I could write a book, but people aren't buying books – certainly not people in foreclosure. When people go into foreclosure, they're in panic mode and they don't understand. They don't know and no one will tell them. The bank won't tell them and their real estate agent won't tell them any of these secrets. Yes, this stuff is simple, it's easy, I can teach it to you very quickly and you can go out and you'll not only be the "knight in shining armor" but you will have all of the tools necessary to be able to do these things: help them!

4415 East Paradise Village Parkway. I'm having a little get-together in a very fancy room here. It's FREE for you and a guest. All you have to do is show up, but you do have to call my assistant Barbara at **1-800-585-3659.** Just let her know what session you like to attend **Saturday at 10:00 a.m. or 2:00 p.m. or Sunday at 10:00 a.m.** or **2:00 p.m.** There's no obligation and when you register we'll be sure to set aside a seat for you. I'll even have a couple free gifts waiting for you.

There is a catch…**seating is extremely limited!** We've sold out the last two seminars we've had in Phoenix. And if you don't register we can not guarantee you a seat and like last time, these usually sell out, so please call right now – 800-585-3659.

But first, here's just a few of the things you'll discover at this special get together this weekend…

- How to fund these deals with O.P.M. (other people's money)
- **Using the secrets I'll show you, people will come out of thing air literally begging you to help them sell their homes**
- How deals will fall into your lap and how to create win-win-win situations and still profit…BIG time
- **Discover the untapped group of homeowners in Phoenix who need your help and how you can collect HUGE, FAT checks**
- And much, much more…

Here's how to get this information in the easiest and simplest way I've ever discovered. Just call Barbara at **1-800-585-3659** and tell her when you'd like to come down – Saturday: 10:00 a.m. or 2:00 p.m. or Sunday: 10:00 a.m. or 2:00 p.m. If you call, I can guarantee that she'll set aside a seat for you and a guest and a gift. It'll be a wonderful afternoon in Scottsdale in a very nice room at The Embassy Suites (4415 East Paradise Village Parkway). There's no dress code. You can dress as comfortably as you want. Parking is free. There's no obligation. You can leave anytime. (Although once you hear how easy and simple these secrets are, I'll bet you remember this day as the first day that your life changed forever, and money became something that was easy to get!)

**To Whom It May Concern:**
*A little over a year ago, Fore-closuresDaily accepted me into their training program. Thanks to ForeclosuresDaily's specific, real world advice, I have now purchased over 14 properties in 14 months, re-selling some of the houses to generate in excess of $100,000 profit, and keeping the rest to start my portfolio of upper-end, middle class rental homes that will serve as the basis for my retirement.*
*Their techniques have allowed me to purchase houses using none of my own credit, and with very little cash down. They have also showed me how to buy houses at 70 percent of their market value (or less). ForeclosuresDaily's training combines extensive experience with plain English instructions, and shows you how to take each step necessary on the path to success. If it weren't for Foreclosures Daily, I'd still be wandering in seminar land. — Sincerely,* **Mark Wilson,** *Tampa, FL*

*"I logged on to foreclosuresdaily.com and identified my target properties. I created a printout of the information, which I used to send out my first set of post-card mailers. And, surprise! I got a call two days later from a motivated seller!… I was told that it takes lots of repeated attempts to get a deal, so I was hardly prepared to handle a sale so quickly. I didn't even have a set of contracts downloaded! After a couple of calls to discount two liens on the property, the deal was closed within about 10 days. We shared a $5,000 assignment fee, which represented 10% of the total equity, and I received my $2,500 check from the title company this week! This may not be the largest sum of money made this year, but it certainly was a fast and fun first deal!" —* **June Butera**

See you on Saturday or Sunday,
Dave VanHoose

**P.S.** You're asking for Barbara at **1-800-585-3659** and be sure to tell her what day (Saturday or Sunday) and time (10:00 a.m. or 2:00 p.m.) you'd like to attend.

**P.P.S.** Don't forget - this is **FREE to attend** and will probably sell out soon! If you just show up without calling, you may not be able to get a seat. If you call first, you definitely have a seat there waiting you and a guest.

**P.P.P.S.** I almost forgot. I have **free gifts** for the first 97 people to register. It's an audio CD resource "How To Find Foreclosures In Your Own Backyard" **valued at $99!**

businesses and acquire customers or clients will unanimously tell you that their success at bringing audiences together comes from doing a lot of different things.

## Where Will YOU Get Your Audiences?

This book is about crafting and delivering presentations—not about seminar or event marketing, so this chapter has barely scratched the surface of that. Speaking Empire has prepared a lengthy, in-depth "Special Report" on Seminar, Workshop, and Special Event Promotion, including samples or promotional pieces. As a reader of this book, you can get a copy free of charge by request.

Simply visit http://nobspresentations.com/bonuses or call 800-687-4061 to request the Special Report on Seminar, Workshop, and Special Event Promotion.

There is a resource system built around Dan Kennedy's seminar marketing strategies called *Butts In Seats: Pack a Room with Your Perfect Audience,* and other related resources available at http://GKIC.com/services/products.

CHAPTER 11

# No Two Audiences Are
## Created Equal

by Dan Kennedy

I am now going to give you a shocking fact about
success with presentations, whether delivered one-to-many
in physical, real-world venues like seminars or delivered
in virtual reality via online media, which we'll next discuss in
Section II of this book. Note I said "success with presentations"—
not "effective presentations."

Here is the shocking fact: Results from a presentation vary,
having *nothing* to do with the presentation itself, its structure, its
content, its cleverness; *nothing* to do with the ability, experience, or
efficacy of the presenter; and *nothing* to do with the venue or the
media where the presentation is delivered. But these variances are
not random or accidental—they are by cause and effect.

This means that everything Dustin, Dave, and I have presented so far about crafting effective presentations is imperiled and potentially sabotaged, even possibly rendered worthless, by this shocking fact if left unmanaged.

There, I said it. This entire book and your time spent with it can be zeroed out by just one mistake.

Almost all my professional speaking, encompassing well over 2,500 compensated engagements plus additional ones done for business promotion, spanning 40 years, have involved my direct selling of print, audio, and video information products in the presentations, driving people to product tables or teams who collect order forms at the back of the room. This is the purest, most honest critique possible. There have been fewer than a dozen of these times when I have zeroed. Blanked. Left empty-handed. Failed abysmally. Not a one of those dozen had anything to do with my presentations; I was delivering already tested, refined, well-proven, and consistently productive presentations. Not a one of those dozen had anything to do with my delivery of the presentations; I was sufficiently rested, healthy, able, prepared, capable, and dynamic. Every one of the dozen "bomb sites" were the result of one thing and one thing only . . .

We are going to talk about **the secret of pre-existing conditions.**

You may know this term from health care and the feature put into the original Obamacare that restricts insurers from refusing coverage or appropriately pricing coverage to people with pre-existing illnesses—making it, incidentally, mathematically and financially impossible to provide health insurance without gigantic financial losses, as the fool's-gold idea invites everybody to wait to buy insurance until they are ill. But this is not the kind of pre-existing condition I'm talking about here, although there are similarities. Not even a newborn infant is free of pre-existing conditions. The baby has genes and thus a genetic predisposition to certain diseases or illnesses and to certain wellness or probable life expectancy. Momma may have smoked, imbibed alcohol, or heaven forbid, listened to rap incessantly and thereby cursed the baby while it was still in its womb. Grown-ups, coming to the doorstep of a health insurer, carry a lot more of these pre-existing conditions. None arrive as pure, clean, and undamaged physical specimens, nor do any arrive with perfectly open, teachable, and coachable minds to be influenced about personal responsibility, diet, or exercise. In the past, insurers were, to some extent, able to sift, sort, reject, and accept people based on both pre-existing conditions and predictive indicators of longevity, years of expensive illness or infirmity, and even compliant or noncompliant behavior. As I write this, that authority over who such companies choose to do business with, at what prices, and under what terms has been largely taken away. This seems like a good thing for consumers, but its evolving reality is collapse of a health insurance system that has served 93% of the American public effectively up until now. Fortunately for you, this authority and power has not been taken from you. You still have the authority and power to choose your customers and your audiences. What I want you to know is how vital it is to exercise that power.

People come into your audience with pre-existing conditions. Mental, emotional, philosophical, experiential, habitual and behavioral, and—important if you are selling—financial. No one comes with a fully open mind or heart. You get no blank slates.

INFORMATION CHANGES LIVES—like nothing else can.

This is the business I am in. I change lives for a living. Mostly, if you craft and deliver presentations, one way or another, you, too, will be in the business of changing lives for a living. If you are a podiatrist and give a presentation all about the history of shoes, the little-understood science of foot health, and the availability of orthotics, you are changing lives by potentially improving the quality of people's lives, extending their ability to participate in sports as recreation in later years, and enabling them to walk, hike, and run without foot pain. If you are a financial advisor, your presentation on minimizing taxes and maximizing yields on safe retirement investments has the potential of giving seniors improved lifestyles, money to aid their grandchildren with college educations, business startups, or first home purchases, more generous contributions to charities, and overall peace of mind. Your presentation may change a retiree from a largely uninformed, vulnerable, and passive investor to a smarter, safer, and more engaged investor. Almost every professional, business owner, and entrepreneur, as well as every author, professional speaker, and self-appointed guru is, by their presentations, attempting to provoke and create change.

After all, who makes any positive change in themselves, their lives, or their businesses without first discovering, being provided, and often being forced to confront information that is new to them?

By presenting information, we are engaged in the noblest of causes. By making people aware of information, ideas, products, and possibilities they never knew existed with well-crafted presentations, we can focus people's attention on beneficial opportunities they would otherwise barely glance at or ignore. When you assemble an audience and deliver your presentation, even when its chief purpose is to acquire a customer or make a sale, you display information that can lead to dynamic change.

But information does not change every life or change any life automatically, organically, or by osmosis. We only affect those ready and willing to be affected. Change is a participatory activity, not a passive receipt. This is why 2, 10, or 10,000 people in very similar circumstances can all be given the same information, and only one or two or a hundred will see any changes because of it. This is why two people in identical businesses in the same town can be given the same information, and one soars to new heights while the other stays in place on the ground. This nearly drove a friend of mine insane: He believed his information should cause everyone he shared it with to soar, and he took each one who didn't personally. The accumulating burden crushed him. I, fortunately, figured it out early and took what some would consider a callous attitude about it: Here is information, do with it what you will or do nothing at all and it's all on you, not me; I will celebrate success with those who use my information, I will ignore, be unfazed by, and do my best to fast forget those who don't.

A change agent can only effect change with change makers. Just as a chef can only create grand meals with the right ingredients, a TV series can succeed only if populated by interesting characters an audience comes to care about, or a car can only get us from place to place fueled with gas and oil—not water and tofu.

This is why psychographics are more important than demographics. This is how data can fail us. I often tell the story about the change in many states' privacy laws years back, which put driver's license data and lists on the market for the first time—giving companies in the diet and weight loss industry the seemingly golden opportunity to get lists by gender, age, height, and weight, thus getting lists of short, fat, dumpy women. It was thought to be a new road to riches. But what the data could not know or tell was whether or not those women cared enough about being dumpy, and were mentally and emotionally ready to responsibly and actively participate in their own positive change.

Information changes lives as nothing else can, but not by itself and not universally applied. The great success philosopher Jim Rohn and I were once comparing notes about many things, and we got to the subject of people whose lives were dramatically changed by our information. Jim pulled several tear-jerking, heart-wrenching, and amazing testimonial letters from his pocket and said, "I've got letters like these filling drawers at home and so do you, and it's important to remember that they have much more to do with the people who wrote them than with me or you." Profoundly true. Jim, quoting from the Bible, taught "If you cast the finest seeds onto hard, infertile ground, nothing will grow. But even the most ordinary seeds cast upon rich, soft, open, fertile ground can grow bountiful crops."

In short, it is the pre-existing conditions of the audience you assemble, appear in front of, or otherwise deliver your presentation to that can, and often does, control your success or disappointing results—not the presentation itself and not your delivery of it.

Even comedians know this to be true. The late, brilliant comedian Shelley Berman often opened his live shows by *instructing* the audience on this fact. He explained that he was performing well-tested and proven funny material just as he had for many other audiences. He told them: "Whether you have a hell of a good time here tonight or not depends a lot more on you than on me."

With all this in mind, there are four very pragmatic, pre-existing condition criteria for you to consider and exercise as much control as possible over for the audiences you deliver your presentations to:

1. **CAN** they buy?
2. **SHOULD** they buy?
3. **WILL** they buy?
4. **CAN** and **WILL** they buy HERE and NOW?

For our purposes here, "buy" can mean "buy," or it can mean some other desired response to and outcome from your presentation.

**CAN** refers mostly to financial ability and secondly to their degree of autonomy in making a decision. If there is a corporate committee, board, accountant, attorney, spouse, etc., with significant influence over the decision to be made, and they are not in the audience right along with your prime target, your presentation is sabotaged. If they have insufficient cash or credit to meet your price for your service or product, the most powerful presentation will fail.

So, here's a trade secret from "get rich in real estate" multi-day boot camps, where training and coaching programs priced from $10,000.00 to $40,000.00 are sold by speakers: Early in the event, a presentation is given about what to say when calling one's credit card companies to get the credit limits on the cards raised, ostensibly to create some working capital for real estate deals. But in harsh reality, this is to enhance the audience members' ability to buy the subsequently offered programs. The attendees are encouraged, on a break in the seminar, to jump on their phones, call their credit card companies, and see what they can get done. You may have a squeamish reaction to this. But it shines a spotlight on how vital the financial ability to buy is. In this case, the wiliest of these marketers not only tries to exert some control over ability to buy—by the media used to attract the people in the first place, the ad messages, and a weeding-out process—but then also tries to better ensure ability to buy during the event where the sales presentation will take place. I am not necessarily suggesting some specific equivalent of this tactic for your business, but I wouldn't rule it out either. I am emphasizing that an audience needs ability to buy to be a receptive, worthwhile audience.

**SHOULD** refers to appropriateness. In my personal opinion, as an example, selling the above-described get-rich-in-real-estate training to truly poor people with hardly any resources, putting them into debt that is significant for them by buying it, and knowing most lack the basic business and negotiating capability required is predatory and dumb business to boot. It is better for that same training be sold to people who are sales professionals in varied fields, owners of home repair and contracting companies, doctors, accountants, and others with a foundational level of capability and the financial wherewithal to support some level of risk. Whatever business you are in, there are people very appropriate for it, marginally appropriate for it, and arguably, mostly inappropriate for it. Granted that every person has the right to judge their own appropriateness. Granted that a super-human salesperson can sell ice makers to Eskimos. But why engage in such difficult work, of questionable value to your audiences and customers or clients and potentially harmful to your own self-esteem, when there are highly appropriate customers for what you have to offer?

**WILL** refers to pre-existing propensity and known, regular behavior. This involves knowing what else they've bought and where, when, and how they bought it, to sync with and avoid acting in opposition to their normal or conditioned behavior. Let me give you an example. I helped launch a now fabulously successful and rather unique software company called Infusionsoft, which has the only fully integrated CRM, online, and offline multistep marketing and no-fail follow-up system for small business. Initially, it was sold from the stage by speakers at my company's member events. It's a complex sale, and early on, it was a largely unknown and unproven product. It involved not only a significant financial commitment but also significant disruption to whatever cobbled-together systems the business owner was already using. I have just described something *not* naturally conducive to a one-step, direct sale by a speaker delivering a presentation to an audience. However, my audiences were well-trained to buy from speakers in such settings and to buy at relatively expensive price points. My audiences were well-conditioned to pay close attention to presentations that obviously had the selling of something as their objective because a reason to be at my company's events was discovery of new and improved business-building tools. The same speaker delivering the same presentation about Infusionsoft would have fallen flat with most other audiences and certainly with an audience assembled on their own of randomly chosen small-business owners. Willingness to buy matters a lot. It segues to . . .

**CAN** AND **WILL** THEY BUY—HERE AND NOW, which refers to the time, place, and circumstances in which your presentation is being delivered as well as to the habitual or conditioned behavior of the audience.

Earlier, Dustin mentioned his dislike of Las Vegas as a site for seminars despite its attractiveness as a destination. I share his position. I believe an audience's ability to buy now can easily be compromised by gambling losses or other impulse expenditures.

And I believe an audience's willingness to buy now can be compromised by being out all night, being hung over, suffering throbbing headaches, and sitting there in a fog. As an aside, for multiday events, I prefer cities with less competition for attention and right-sized, somewhat isolated hotels where my audience takes the property over, stays on-site on breaks and after hours, and convenes together in the restaurant and bar rather than scattering to the four winds.

Different people have different propensity for decisive action or purchasing. Entrepreneurs, for example, tend to make immediate decisions more readily than do corporate executives. Salespeople tend to make immediate decisions more readily than engineers or school teachers. Obviously, as noted in the Infusionsoft example, people experienced in buying from group presentations are more likely to buy from group presentations than are virgins with no such experience.

So, with all this said, it is incumbent on you not to simply assemble any audience or to accept opportunities to deliver your presentation to any audience but to be strategic and thoughtful about the makeup of the audience. Only by exerting control over pre-existing conditions of your audience can you fully profit from a great presentation.

# PRESENTATIONS AND
# ONLINE MEDIA

# CHAPTER 12

# The Power of Webinars and Online Media
## How to Speak While You Sleep

by Dustin Mathews

For a long *time, your only real use of* a powerful presentation was for manual labor. Speakers traveled from city to city to deliver their presentations at others' organized meetings, at churches, at hotel ballrooms, and at convention centers—basically, anywhere we could find, assemble, borrow, or rent an audience. P.T. Barnum did it, lecturing on The Art of Money-Getting. Mark Twain did it. Today, authors, professional speakers, promoters of various kinds of opportunities, reality TV stars, corporate trainers, and consultants still hit the road regularly, taking their presentation to audiences. At the local level, doctors, lawyers, accountants, investment advisors, and other professionals and business owners go out to civic groups, business groups, and luncheons; advertise and promote their own seminars and introductory classes; and maybe go into companies and do lunch-and-learn sessions for the host's employees, always taking their presentations to audiences. But what if you could bring the audience to the presentation?

We remain fans of the "old school" way. It works. Most of the time, it works better than anything done online with the same presentation by any tangible measurement: sales made, customers obtained, appointments booked. There is, however, a very significant expense of money and time involved when going around the country or the globe, or even just around your city, to deliver your presentation. There are also people who will never set foot in a free preview seminar, come to an "executive briefing," or otherwise place themselves in an audience, but these same people may be great prospects for your business.

This is where online media becomes so valuable. If you have a presentation that works, perfected with live audiences in the flesh, there's a 99% likelihood it can be made to work as-is or adapted as a *webinar*—short for "seminar delivered on the web." This lets you speak while you sleep. It lets you reach audiences you wouldn't in person. It multiplies the value of your presentation. It allows an audience of one to watch your presentation whenever he wants to, on demand, just like he watches movies, TV shows, and/or replays of sports games. It allows you to push a group to watch it at a designated date and time, just as you would if traveling to Boston and holding a meeting in a hotel. It is versatile, efficient, and can be entirely automated.

At Speaking Empire, we've helped thousands of people convert effective presentations into effective webinars and build marketing systems around them. This includes people who want to reach a national or global audience like authors, consultants, and thought leaders. It also includes the dentist, cosmetic dentist, cosmetic surgeon, investment advisor, real estate agent, school owner, interior designer, etc., etc., operating a business in a local market, who can benefit by having a presentation they do to small groups invited into their offices or to civic or business club groups available to any size audience—even an audience of one, online, on demand, in a self-operating theater. As we did with The Speaking Formula, we developed The Ultimate Webinar Formula (see Figure 12.1).

## 1: Traffic

Just as you or somebody has to invite and motivate people to come to a meeting at a physical location, you have to invite and motivate your audience to come and watch your webinar. There is certainly no shortage of ways to do this. There is email, social media, offline direct mail, ads in magazines, even radio and TV,

**FIGURE 12.1:** The Ultimate Webinar Formula

The **ULTIMATE**
Webinar Formula

1 • **Drive Traffic**
2 • **Register 'Em**
3 • **Build Excitement**
4 • **Deliver Your Signature Presentation** (Hot List)
5 • **Follow Up Like Crazy**
6 • **Stick & Over***deliver*

and opportunities to get other people to promote your webinar for you, for affiliate commissions or for reciprocity of some kind or just because they know you and like you.

If you'd like to see a sample email sequence we've used for our own business and get more information about bringing audiences to your webinar, go to http://NoBSPresentations. com/traffic for free resources.

## 2: Registration

It's rare that you want to set up a webinar for direct, on-demand access without some sort of registration. People are used to registering for seminars and classes, so there's very little resistance. You want this list for follow-up. Figure 12.2 on page 101 shows an example of one of our registration pages.

As you can see, there's a headline, a photo of the presenter, and a little sales copy about what you would learn if watching. You'll also see a countdown timer. In Chapter 5 about our Irresistible Offer Architecture®, we talked about deadlines and urgency. The clock here is literally ticking! It's counting down to the moment when this webinar will not be available any longer.

## 3: Build Excitement

First of all, you don't want to take enthusiasm or follow-through on people's part for granted. That's why there's sales copy on the registration page. If there's a delay between registration and the webinar (or a live webcast), there should be a series of follow-up messages by email and text, possibly voice broadcast, and possibly mail to build their interest in the upcoming webinar. Much of the time, getting a person

**FIGURE 12.2:** Registration Page

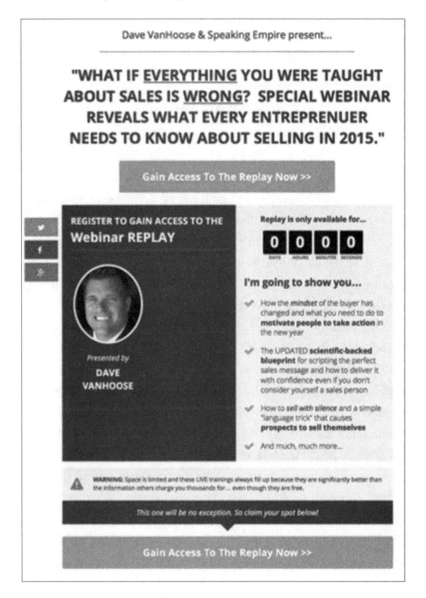

registered is the start of a process—not the end of it. We have to sell people who've registered on showing up! The good news is, just as with the playing and replaying of the webinar itself, all this communication can be automated.

## 4: The Presentation

This is the easy part. You just have to deliver your Signature Presentation that you perfected based on the advice in this book and (ideally) battle-tested with live audiences. It can be a completely prerecorded video, or it can be done live as a webcast. If it is to work while you sleep, it's obviously prerecorded. There are things you can do with a webinar that are impractical for presentations in physical locations, especially if traveling to various sites to deliver your presentation, and Dan Kennedy discusses those in the next chapter.

One important difference is that you can't stampede people to the back of the room to sign up for or buy whatever you are offering. Instead, you will most likely want to direct your audience to what we call a "Hot List" page. This is a separate website you'll direct them to or have them click to, where they opt-in again, then move on to enrolling or ordering or scheduling with you. We split the requesting of their contact information and then their purchase information into two opt-in pages, like the ones in Figures 12.3 and 12.4 on page 103, so that when someone leaves without completing the purchase, we know to follow up with them in a certain way. This is our new list of hot prospects. At times, you might add as an option or even substitute calling your business or an outsourced call center.

**FIGURE 12.3:** Hot List Opt-In Page

**FIGURE 12.4:** Opt-In Page

## 5: Follow Up . . . Like Crazy!

Your webinar becomes the center of a lot of follow-up marketing activity. It creates different lists of people for different kinds of follow-up marketing:

- Everyone that buys or takes whatever substitute action you're asking for
- Everyone on the Hot List who doesn't complete their purchase or action
- Everyone who watched the webinar but did not go to the Hot List
- Everyone who registered but did not attend/watch the webinar

In addition to your own direct follow-up by email, text, mail, and phone, you can do automated retargeting with Facebook and Google. A follow-up message can literally follow the person around. For more details about this, check out the information and resources at http://NoBSPresentations.com/perfectaudience.

## 6: Stick and Overdeliver

Whether you use your webinar to sell a product or get people to request free information or schedule an appointment, you want to immediately email them a confirmation of what they did, verification of what is coming to them, and, if it was a purchase, a receipt. In some cases, this can also be used to offer an immediate upsell to a deluxe or bigger version of what they just bought or to set up a second, sequential sale. Now, more than ever, people want instant gratification, so even if your product is physical (not digital) and will be shipped to them, or they've made an appointment for a phone consultation or to come into your office, showroom, or store some time from now, it's good to give them something extra they can consume immediately. This might be an educational video, a downloadable information item, a membership site—*something*.

People who buy something from Speaking Empire online also get offline touches—an old-fashioned, handwritten thank-you note and some kind of printed CD or DVD deliverable. One reason for this is that our typical customer is a boomer or senior, but regardless, I want them to have a great experience, and nothing is quite like getting and opening a package.

When you move your effective presentation online and wrap these six results boosters around it, you leverage that presentation to a much greater extent than you could by just packing your duffel bag with a change of clothes and laptop loaded with your PowerPoint slides and playing Have Speech, Will Travel.

# CHAPTER 13

# It's TV

by Dan Kennedy

*hen they watch it on a screen, it's TV.*

In the last chapter, Dustin brilliantly laid out his Webinar Formula. I want to go back in and talk about the presentation itself delivered by the webinar. First, though, I have an important, broader point to make about what he just explained. It has to do with the difference between *doing* things and *owning* things. When you are a speaker or presenter delivering a presentation, you are a laborer doing things. It can be high-paid labor, but that's still what it is. It can only produce income. And it is just as dependent on you being healthy, able, and willing to report to work as the convenience store clerk's paycheck is dependent on him trudging in on time every day.

When you convert a powerful presentation to a webinar and put in place a system to drive an audience to it, you own what I call a *Marketing Asset*. You get income from doing things. You get wealth, independence, and security from owning things.

---

For a thorough and complete understanding of Direct-Marketing Assets, and of Kennedy approaches to marketing, start with Dan's book *No B.S. Guide to DIRECT Marketing for NON-Direct Marketing Businesses, 2nd Edition.* Also, visit http://NoBSBooks.com and http://GKIC.com.

For more from Dan on the subject of wealth, get the book *No B.S. Wealth Attraction In The New Economy.*

---

Returning to the presentation itself, and the relocation of it to online media, there are two big secrets of mine to consider and keep in mind.

**First Secret: When they watch it on a screen, it's TV.** I've done a great deal of work over many years with aired-on-TV half-hour infomercials—for information products and courses, for free preview seminars occurring in various cities, for moneymaking opportunities, for skin-care and cosmetic products, weight loss and fitness products, and a wide array of other products and services. My longest tenured client is a Very Big Dog in that industry: the Guthy-Renker corporation, known for everything from the original Tony Robbins infomercials to its biggest, flagship skin-care brand, Proactiv®. I've worked with them since 1988. I learned as I went, as I came to writing, developing, and even producing infomercials only with direct-response advertising experience but no experience with TV or video production. I made quite a name for myself. I even have a show entirely of my invention and production that set and still holds the record for the longest uninterrupted airing for a lead-generation infomercial in its category: every day and every night for eight years. What I learned about the viewer and what works best to get and hold his attention, build interest, and get him off the couch and to the phone with infomercials has given me a unique advantage in writing and producing video for webinars. This information can also be used inside offices such as professional practices or on DVDs sent to prospects, and in creating and producing live webcasts. I always think of it as TV.

People have certain expectations about TV. There are certain formats they are very familiar with, expect, have been conditioned to accept, and are eager to give attention to. News broadcasts, daytime talk shows, and cable news talk shows have definitive looks, feels, and choreography to them. This makes the set very important. Most news and news-talk shows now have type streaming across the bottom of the screen, graphics—like "Breaking News"—and often big screens where video or charts and graphs are shown. When a viewer finds himself watching that, he knows he is watching a news program. Daytime talk shows like *Ellen* usually have more of a living room feel to them. Morning programs like *The Today Show* have different segments at different kinds of sets—news, living room, kitchen. Most TV has a lot of activity and movement to it. The very static two people across a desk show like Larry King or Charlie Rose is nearly dead. You will occasionally see an infomercial done this way, because it's cheap to do, but you won't catch any major player using that format. People expect things to happen on TV.

At GKIC, the company I founded and that is built around me, we perfected a format and formula for new information product launches with a series of brief excitement-building videos, then a four-hour live webcast (often with me), a host, and sometimes other guests. The webcasts are divided into three segments exactly like an infomercial is with prerecorded commercials for the offered product inserted at three breaks. Each of these webinar/webcast "events" has generated from hundreds of thousands to over a million dollars in revenue. Several different sets were used throughout the three-year series, always with an eye to it being watched as if TV.

It would be very rare for me to simply take a speaker or presenter who has been delivering a stand-up presentation successfully, film him doing it, and air that online as a webinar. It's done, and I have done it, but there have to be very special circumstances supporting it, notably its use only for a very dedicated audience or with an extraordinarily charismatic and attention-commanding star of the show. I was involved with this with a famous weight loss infomercial, *Stop the Insanity!* featuring the crew-cut, tall, lanky, screaming Susan Powter. The show was well-produced by a guy named Packy McFarland but simple: a live audience seated in three-quarter-round, Susan on stage, and her frenzied performance. It was hard to take your eyes off of it. In most cases, I'm going to take the proven presentation and take it apart and re-assemble it to be delivered as a TV show.

**The Second Secret** about online media delivery in place of in-person, in-a-physical-room delivery **is that there are a lot of things you can do online that are impractical or too costly to do in a live presentation**, especially if occurring dozens or hundreds of times a year in different locations and venues—but even if it's an implant dentistry introductory seminar done just once a month for a small audience squeezed into your dental office's reception room. For example, consider testimonials. It's great at a live presentation to have your three or four most enthusiastic, most articulate customers, clients, or patients present, to be stood up or brought up on stage, and to be interviewed by you or to tell their before-and-after story. But they probably are not going to get on your bus and travel with you to 20 different cities, and even if they did, they'd tire of performing and become less and less effective. Even for that dentist doing six, eight, or ten in-office seminars a year, getting those same star patients to come and sing 'n' dance at all of them isn't practical. Unfortunately, in live presentations, audiences tend to tune out when made to watch video. Some even resent it. With a webinar, however, they are already watching TV, and cutting away to a brief video testimonial is like having Jimmy Fallon and a guest cut to a clip of the guest's movie. You can immortalize your star customer telling his story most enthusiastically, possibly on location on the yacht he bought with the money he made with your system or in the kitchen merrily cooking while talking about the classes he took at the cooking school you run in the back of your kitchenware store. You get to have him appear in your webinar 10, 100, or 1,000 times and he never gets tired—fresh as a daisy every time.

There are also all kinds of on-screen graphics, split-screen images, PowerPoint slides with voice-over, physical demonstrations filmed in real-life situations rather than inside a seminar room, and other effects we can do to enhance the webinar that can't be done during a live, stand-up presentation. Earlier in this book, Dave mentioned the seven-minute attention span. He's probably generous. When I put together a video for airing online or to be sent to a prospect, I like to mix up what they're seeing on screen every three to seven minutes.

In videos I produced for a group of orthodontic practices, to be shown in-office, sent on DVD, aired at the doctors' websites and on YouTube, in different ones, I utilized a Rolls-Royce, a classic sports car, and a stunt dog, as well as two sets and a plethora of on-screen graphics. No doctor is going to bring two cars and a dog into his office or to a local hotel meeting room for his presentation. (These videos are used by www. ExcellenceInOrthodontics.org.)

Depending on the size and scope of your business, anticipated length or frequency of use of your webinar or video, or anticipated audience size, you can also involve a rented celebrity host. I have produced videos for online and delivery to prospects for a consulting company in the hospital industry using tennis champion Chris Evert, for a health-care practice using Rose Marie (*The Dick Van Dyke Show*), for a financial services company with football champion Rocky Bleier, and many others.

Remember, I am creating Marketing Assets—not one-'n'-done presentations.

And remember, all of this is about leveraging a proven, powerful presentation that works delivered live and in person to audiences. This is about marrying and merging that presentation with the techniques and formats of direct-response TV infomercials to wind up with effective webinars, video sales letters, or even live webcasts.

**This brings me to a third and final point:** *leverage*. When you have a powerful, effective presentation, you want to use it in as many different ways and as many different media as possible. I love working with a client who has a great presentation. It or pieces of it can become sales letters and literature for direct mail, a book, or books for authority and "thud impact," and lead-generating bait, audio CDs, DVDs, and more. Material can also be repurposed for lead generation, making a sale, and follow-up in appointment, no-sale situations. The one power presentation becomes the foundation for a plethora of media and the Copy Bank from which, as the copywriter, I can make withdrawals to serve as starting points, themes, or basis for an entire portfolio of Marketing Assets.

In my consulting and copywriting practice, I am usually developing complex, multimedia, multistep, front-end (customer/client/patient acquisition), and back-end (unconverted lead and customer monetization) systems. Most businesses have operating systems—out of necessity—but few have real marketing systems. Instead, they have random and erratic acts, advertising disconnected from marketing, and marketing disconnected from selling, poor use of media in place of manual labor (exactly what we've been talking about here in Chapters 12 and 13), and a lot of ideas they can't get implemented. Leverage is in Systems. If there's reason for you to communicate with me directly about development of Marketing Systems for your business, you can do so by fax: (602) 269-3113.

# CHAPTER 14

# StealthSeminar
## Automate Your Presentations and Profits

by Special Guest Expert Geoff Ronning

Top income business owners, private practice professionals, and sales pros as well as authors, speakers, and consultants share a secret: automation. As many things that work for them as possible get put on autopilot. The powerful, effective presentation fits this perfectly. I built a technology and tech service for this purpose called StealthSeminar. Dustin and Dave invited me to present it in this book because they knew you would get excited about using automated webinars but then wonder: How can I get all this done?

## What Is StealthSeminar?

StealthSeminar is the longest running automated webinar software available. An automated webinar is a webinar that is delivered to your prospects and clients on autopilot. It is set to run automatically so you can be working on other projects, playing golf, cruising the Caribbean with your family, or doing any other activities requiring your attention. The webinar runs automatically—your manual labor isn't required.

## Why StealthSeminar?

There are a number of benefits to using StealthSeminar, including the following.

### *Build Your Lead List*

Collecting lead data is getting harder and harder. Having them opt into a webinar is a great way to acquire your lead information in a simple, powerful fashion. People are used to registering for events. Using a webinar quickly builds your list and allows you to do so effortlessly.

### *Scale Your Business*

Using StealthSeminar, you can scale your business with automation. If you are relying on your manual efforts each time to give a presentation or webcast, you are limiting the number of times you can deliver your presentation. Through automation, you can run your webinar as many times as you deem fit each and every day.

### *Offer Convenient Times for Your Leads and Clients*

Business is worldwide. Time zones can be tricky to navigate. Allowing your webinar to run at the times your attendees want to watch will increase your registrants and allow you to cater to their needs without working 24/7.

## No Presentation Pressure or Fear

Many people have a fear of public speaking. By creating a webinar and using StealthSeminar, you remove the public speaking factor. You record the webinar in a controlled, comfortable environment so you don't have any fears or pressure. You then just upload that video to run as an automated webinar.

## No Relying on Your Health or Mood

When you present a live seminar, it is easy for day-to-day frustrations and challenges to come through. For instance, if you have a sore throat, it's hard to hide that while sucking on cough drops. Or, if you had a sick child or spouse that kept you up all night, or if you are ill yourself, the lack of sleep and sickness is easily seen by your audience.

In addition, if you have had a bad day or are frustrated by something, that can also impact your performance. By automating your webinar, you are providing the same crisp, fresh presentation each and every time it runs.

## Always Present Your Highest Converting Presentation

With StealthSeminar, you can always be sure you are going to be presenting the most valuable webinar because you do something called "split testing." Split testing allows you to play one presentation to one group of individuals while playing a second presentation to another group. By doing this, you can look at the statistics and see what presentation converts the highest and achieves the goals you're looking to achieve. You are automatically improving your success on a daily basis.

### *No Technical Snafus*

Presenting live webinars requires a healthy computer as well as a strong internet connection. If there are any issues with either one of those during your webinar, your event is impacted, and potentially, your audience lost. With StealthSeminar, the technical requirements are far less because you are not actually broadcasting your webinar. Therefore, it's much easier and much more reliable.

### *Laser-Sharp Follow-Up to Maximize Your Conversions*

You can track who showed up for your webinars, as well as how long they stayed and deliver messages that match the needs of each individual attendee. If they register but don't show up, you speak to that individual. If they show up but leave early, you deliver that message. If they stay the entire time but don't convert, you give them what they need to convert. If they show up and convert, you deliver a message to ensure their satisfaction. Throughout the entire process, you control and optimize the experience for your attendees so they convert at the highest levels possible.

## What Does a StealthSeminar Webinar Look Like?

A StealthSeminar webinar looks exactly like you would expect a live webinar to look. The key to the highest-converting webinar is the interaction by the attendees, albeit automated. You accomplish that by using a chat box (which is fully controlled through automation), calls to actions that appear and disappear, countdown timers, etc., all under your control and set up when your seminar is launched on StealthSeminar. See Figure 14.1 on page 119.

FIGURE **14.1:** Ronning Webinar Prosperity Segmentation

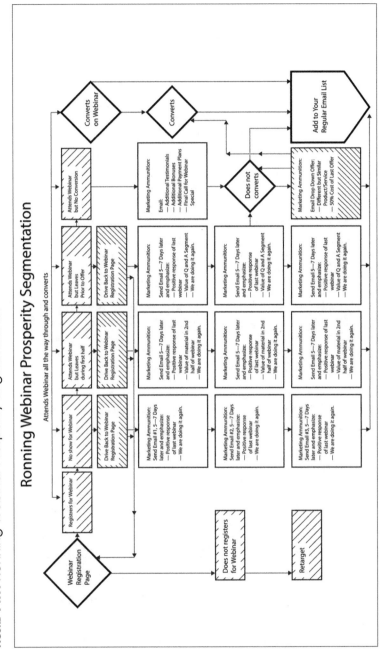

Ronning Webinar Prosperity Segmentation

Should you not want to use all those bells and whistles, you can also choose to not do so. You are in full control and can set it up as you see fit.

## Is Using StealthSeminar Ethical?

I would never tell you what is ethical for you. However, I will tell you that there are a lot of ways to present a webinar on StealthSeminar. For instance, some people choose to present a webinar exactly as if it is live and tell their viewers it is live. Others choose to tell people it is not live. I personally choose to deliver the webinar and allow the attendees to come to their own conclusions. I don't say it is live; I don't say it isn't.

There are a lot of automation tools that I use that do the exact same thing—for instance, with an autoresponder sequence, I do not start off the email telling people that I wrote this on December 4, 2010. I let the message speak for itself.

By not saying it's live and allowing them to come to their own conclusions, I feel comfortable. Again, it is a personal decision and you should do what you are comfortable doing. In either case, saying it is live, not commenting on it, or saying it is recorded is fine.

## Automated Webinars versus Live Webinars

A lot of times, people wonder if live webinars convert better than automated webinars. The answer for a lot of people is that live webinars work better. Then again, for some people, automated webinars work much better. It's no surprise why; an automated webinar allows you to make the same sharp presentation each and every time in any time zone.

But it gets even better when it comes to leveraging time and scaling a business. When you consider the time freed up by automating your webinar, there is no comparison. Automated is the runaway winner.

Many StealthSeminar clients are running a dozen or more webinars a day. Some are running hundreds a day. So, even if their conversion rate is slightly lower versus live, the quantity of automated webinars they are doing is far, far more profitable than the limited number of webinars they can do live.

There is no comparison to what you can do live versus automated.

## Types of StealthSeminar Events

There is no limit to the types of events you can create. Do you want more leads? You can automate it. Do you want more sales? You can generate them daily. Do you want to deliver paid content on autopilot? Done. Bonuses? Great. People are using StealthSeminar in all aspects of their business.

Let's look closer at three different case studies: a strategy session close, a direct product sale, and one in the financial industry.

### *The Strategy Session Close*

In more complex sales, it helps to speak to someone personally. These types of sales usually involve higher-ticket items or a lot of delivery variables.

CASE STUDY: STRATEGY SESSION WEBINAR

ORGANIZATION: CLIENTS ON DEMAND™

Russell Ruffino is the entrepreneur behind Clients on Demand™. Ruffino is one of today's most successful internet marketing gurus.

## THE CHALLENGE

His business success depends on generating leads, establishing trust, and qualifying them to guide those that are appropriate to the next step—a Strategy Session on the phone. Ruffino experimented with all different types of lead-generation strategies to achieve those goals, including downloads, mind maps, minicourses, videos, and even a book. They were doing well but not as well as he wanted.

Then, he tested an automated webinar. The webinar became his most successful strategy up to that point. His business was growing, but it was not doing what it should have been doing.

The automated webinar software he was testing was not StealthSeminar. He noticed the other automated webinar systems he tried were not stable. Sometimes they worked, sometimes they didn't.

In addition, he noticed none of the other automated webinar software converted for mobile traffic, **which now makes up 51%** of all traffic. StealthSeminar alone is the only one that runs webinars correctly on iPhone. All others show a video length and fast forward button. That isn't good if you want to control how your attendees consume the content.

## THE SOLUTION

Russell Ruffino tried StealthSeminar. He was amazed with the results. His business soared 1503.33% initially using Stealth-Seminar and since then, much more (see Figure14.2 on page 123).

Ruffino has found the best way to connect with potential clients, build trust, and qualify them is via a StealthSeminar.

He has a fantastic webinar that his attendees love. During the webinar, the attendees, who have no previous knowledge of Ruffino, are introduced to him and his system. Ruffino provides terrific content, builds trust, makes the connection with each

**FIGURE 14.2:** Comparing Results

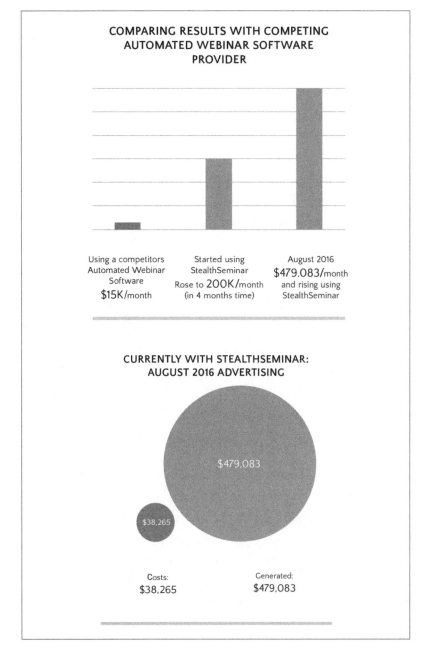

CHAPTER 14 / STEALTHSEMINAR

attendee, and then drives those who are qualified to make an appointment. A link appears for the attendees to click on to set an appointment for a Strategy Session.

On the Strategy Session, the prospect learns more about the program and is further qualified. If the match is appropriate, the offer is made for the individual to join Russell Ruffino and Clients on Demand.

## *The Direct-Sale Webinar*

In simpler sales, speaking to someone is not required and often can cost you sales. These types of sales typically run from $47.00 to $2,500.00. The sweet spot for direct-sales webinars is $197.00 to $1,497.00.

### CASE STUDY: DIRECT-SALE WEBINAR
### ORGANIZATION: FOREXTRADING HISPANO

Christian Helmut is the driving force behind Alfonso & Christian (http://AlfonsoyChristian.com/blog). They are business growth consultants running multiple businesses and multiple different webinar types. They help people scale and automate their processes. Lets look at a direct-sale webinar.

### THE CHALLENGE

Christian Helmut wanted to automate the sales cycle process. In addition, his company wanted to provide value and position itself as the best inside the marketplace—all that without human intervention.

Helmut and his colleagues tried different ways to generate leads and establish their expert positioning. While successful, it did not satisfy the goals they had set for themselves.

They were not getting the number of leads they wanted at an acceptable cost to them. They also weren't selling the amount of products that they knew they could.

## THE SOLUTION

Christian Helmut then tested StealthSeminar. He created an automated webinar. They started to drive cold traffic from Facebook and YouTube video ads to their automated webinar.

Helmut's list started to grow rapidly. Their positioning reached the top of the marketplace. The automated webinar started to generate sales on autopilot. In fact, they are getting a 15x ROI. For every $1.00 they spend, they get back $15.00—all automated.

### *The Financial Industry Webinar*

The financial industry is also being heavily impacted by automated webinars. In the past, a lot of individuals would do seminars in a live setting, such as a restaurant or hotel. Now it is getting harder and more costly to get people to attend such events. The online webinar allows you to reach those individuals much cheaper and make it much more convenient for them to attend from their home or office.

CASE STUDY: FINANCIAL INDUSTRY WEBINAR

ORGANIZATION: ANNUITYCHECK™

Steve Hutchinson is the founder of AnnuityCheck™ (www. annuitycheck.com). He has a lifetime of experience in the financial industry, and he wanted to maximize his success with AnnuityCheck, a SaaS fintech firm.

## THE CHALLENGE

Steve Hutchinson wanted to help financial advisers automate their financial calculations and maximize the retirement income they generated for their clients.

He spent the first two years doing live webinars. He would waste 10 to 20 hours every week getting prepped for one or two webinars. It was wasteful and a drain on him mentally and physically. It took away from other professional and personal activities.

## THE SOLUTION

Hutchinson finally turned to automation via StealthSeminar for his webinars.

Hutchinson found a "whole new marketing gear" in online optimization. He finally turned to the same type of automation his clients depend upon to streamline the process. "Now I can update a simple file a few times a month as needed and get my life back," says Hutchinson.

AnnuityCheck did their first two automated webinars on a Friday through Sunday and Monday. The statistics show they had 538 registrations, 272 attendees, and 46 signed up with credit card—17%.

As you can see, there are a lot of benefits to creating your own automated webinars. They are a powerful tool that can be used for many different applications, such as list building, generating leads, or converting sales. Get started today. Every day you wait is costing you precious time and business. Getting your webinar up and running is easy to do. I wish you much success!

Geoff Ronning is cofounder of StealthSeminar (www.stealthseminar.com) and FreeWebinarSchool (www.freewebinarschool.com). He and his team have a front-row seat and advisory role to webinars that are running around the world. They have observed over 9 million webinar attendees. That gives them data, knowledge, and information that no one has about webinars. Geoff Ronning can help you grow your business with one of the most powerful marketing tools available, StealthSeminar.

# FOLLOW-UP TO PRESENTATIONS

# CHAPTER 15

# Turning Leftovers into
## Rich Meals

by Dan Kennedy

Y ou can often make a pretty good meal, or two or three, out of leftovers. If you have ever been relatively poor, or your family was poor when you were a kid, you definitely know about soup or stew full of leftovers from several prior days' meals as a meal. Everybody turns Thanksgiving feast leftovers into a night of sandwiches and another night of open-faced turkey sandwiches with gravy.

Presentations leave leftovers on the table, too.

There are people who expressed interest but never registered online—at your website, or by calling your office. There are people who registered to attend or watch but failed to show up. There are the people who showed up but failed to buy or take another desired action. There can be recoverable value in all of those lists.

Sometimes, monetization can be a simple matter of somehow giving them the same presentation again. For a TV infomercial client, I took all the people calling in but bailing out of the conversation with the order-taker before buying and sent them a letter with an audio recording of the very same infomercial they had watched. This converted more than enough of these nonbuyers to buyers to be nicely profitable. For most of the nine years that I spoke on America's number-one seminar tour, SUCCESS, usually as the last speaker of the day, I came home and mailed a very long letter essentially transcribed from my presentation to all the ticket buyers who had not bought my resources. Many had not stayed all the way to the long day's end to even see me at all. Others were, by then, spent out, lugging bags of other speakers' resources. This follow-up mailing never failed to be satisfactorily profitable, and it brought thousands of new customers into my world who would have been left behind otherwise. Similarly, during the several years that I did a lot of consulting with Weight Watchers International, Inc., I determined that people going to introductory meetings and getting the initial presentation but not joining were getting little or no follow-up, and I proved that an immediate follow-up letter built around the presentation sent the next day by Federal Express got a large number of those people to join.

Other times, more complex and sophisticated follow-up can be warranted. I have a longtime client who sells a service to dentists via a presentation delivered live and in person in seminars and online by a webinar. The doctors attending the seminars or watching the online presentations who do not sign up for the service get not one but three sequential follow-up campaigns, each with 16 to 32 steps, incorporating mail, email, and phone, over eight to ten weeks. The first campaign offers the same service by restating the same presentation carved into pieces. The second campaign offers a stripped-down version of the same service at a lower price. The third campaign offers an entirely different service and drives to a different online presentation to sell it. You should brace yourself for the piece of insider's information I'm going to share with you: The profit from eating these leftovers is almost identical to the profit from the primary presentation and its sales. In other words, we nearly doubled the income from the same audience by this follow-up.

This is not a freak situation. To the contrary, I usually find some opportunity to make good meals out of leftovers, with just about every client I work with, by follow-up, often recycling the same presentation or at least the elements and content of the original presentation. Based on this, in acting as your own consultant, you have two questions to give a lot of consideration to:

1. Where are leftovers being tossed in the trash, rather than being used to make meals?
2. How many times, places, and ways can I reuse or recycle my effective presentations?

During two years that I was coaching a group of high-income, top-performing financial advisors who all obtained clients by assembling audiences for their own preview seminars, I asked: What do you do with all the people who attend these seminars but don't book private appointments with y'all? Given the success of these advisors, I got surprisingly poor answers: One said sheepishly, "Nothing much." Two, "We put them back into our prospect list"—which meant they got future mailings (only) for the same seminar they'd already attended and failed to act on. Three, "If Harriet has time, she calls them." And how often would you guess that Harriet has time to call them? We developed a 16-step, 8-week follow-up system, using mail and email, entirely automated, and saw conversion rates as high as 25%. This follow-up message leveraged the content of the original presentation.

Good telephone follow-up almost always pays, and Dustin tackles this in the next chapter.

To paint a total picture, your presentation should never be a stand-alone item. It has a place inside a business building or marketing system with steps occurring ahead of the presentation and steps occurring behind the presentation.

While this book has focused on the presentation, the reality is that the depository of all the financial value is the customer and the potential customer, prospect, and lead. These unconverted prospects contain gold like cactuses contain water—it isn't obviously visible, but it *is* there.

# CHAPTER 16

# The Post-Presentation
## Conversation

by Dustin Mathews

Although we do a lot of follow-up by mail, email, retargeting with social media, newsletters, and other means, including in sequences like Dan just described, I find nothing trumps a one-to-one telephone conversation with a friendly, competent person conducting the call. We have developed a very effective template for these calls. With some adjustments, it would be a good template for you too. I don't want you to undervalue this. If you hired a sales script writer to develop this kind of thing for you, it'd be easy to spend $5,000.00 to $10,000.00.

When you add this process, you are, with those not buying at your presentation, using that fact and the presentation as a very good excuse or reason for the post-presentation phone conversation. Anytime you can have a conversation with a qualified prospect, that's a good thing, but as you certainly know, there is a high level of resistance to telemarketing calls. In these cases, the calls don't have to be perceived as telemarketing, and there is a relationship of sorts in place in advance of the call. This is a very different dynamic than a typical telemarketing call.

It is definitely best to get every sale you can at your presentation—nothing beats NOW. But if you have what Dan called leftovers to try and make a meal from, here are follow-up questions:

1. *We appreciate your having attended Dave's presentation. Thank you. Could I ask you a few questions about your thoughts about the presentation?*

   We ask this question to get people into the Yes State that Dave talked about earlier in the book. It's an easy way to start. It sounds like the call is more of a survey call than a sales call.

2. *What were some of the things you liked most or found most interesting about Dave's presentation?*

   We ask this to put them back into the time when they were excited. You should notice that the question is framed to encourage a positive response.

3. *Dave is very particular about who he works with. He likes working with people doing something important, so please tell me how your business positively impacts people and might even change the world?*

   People tend to enter sales conversations trying to sell. We take an interview approach instead. With a question like this, we turn the tables and get the prospect to sell us rather than us selling them. This question also gives the prospect an opportunity to talk about his business in glowing terms.

4. *What's your "bigger reason" for being in your business and doing what you do? Do you have a legacy in mind to create?*

This lets people know we're not just there to sell; we truly want to help people build a legacy for themselves and have their business and life mean something. We've learned that buying and price resistance goes down when people are focused on "deeper meanings." This also challenges people to think bigger.

5. *What's your greatest challenge?*

This starts movement toward offering our assistance. Depending on the answer, we have two immediate follow-up questions: What about that is your biggest problem? And: What is it costing you? These are pain-inducing questions to establish a disease we can cure.

6. *Do you have a budget to solve this problem?*

This raises the issue of money so you can try to understand where the person is financially. In our business, we have different versions of our services that we can prescribe, at different prices, so getting a sense of the person's ideas about acceptable price is very useful. An alternative or follow-up question is: What do you think it could be worth for you to solve this problem?

7. *Based on Dave's presentation and what you know about Speaking Empire, how do you think what we do might help you the most?*

This is a key question. Given answers to questions 5 and 6, most salespeople would jump ahead to selling a solution. We prefer to get the prospect to tell us how they think we can help them—essentially selling themselves. This reduces the stress of the conversation. It also allows less skilled salespeople to conduct these conversations.

8. *Would it be OK if I continue with that, and share how I think we can help you?*

This returns control to us, in a friendly way. It's at this point that I am going to lay out a couple, or at most three, options for work with our company on a project, leading to . . .

9. *Which option works best for you?*

Because we structured an either/or alternate choice instead of a yes/no, most people who have gone this far will pick one of the options, or at least pick one to ask additional questions about. After answering any such questions and getting a choice made, we usually offer a post-event discount or bonus or both . . .

10. *The good news is that we have a post-event special offer for this . . .*

From here, we move into getting the order written.

Now, a confession of sorts. In our business, at most of our multiday events, we actually use this template—slightly tweaked—to sit down with prospects right then and there and close our sales immediately. This is how our on-site salespeople carry on their conversations with each person in attendance.

We want to fully capitalize on the excitement and energy of the moment. But, as I've shown here, the very same template can be used for post-event or post-presentation follow-up on phone calls.

CHAPTER 17

# The Best Story Wins—or
## Does It?

by Dan Kennedy

W hat has this book really been about?
Presentations? Storytelling? Persuasion? Process?
All those things.

Certainly, a great presentation tells a great story: a story about your business, practice, or charity. About you and why and how you do what you do. A story in which your customer or potential customer stars and sees himself starring. So, do the best stories win? A chief point of this book is: It's not that simple.

One of many good and important books about storytelling is Annette Simmons' *Whoever Tells the Best Story Wins*.

There are many kinds of stories. There is the overarching, life-evolving narrative of a person, place, business, or product. There are stories adapted for different audiences, different purposes, and different times. There are stories that influence, stories that bond, stories that outright sell. Most of the time in most competitive situations—even if only competing for an audience's attention in an attention deficit disorder world—it is the best story that wins. Yet that is deceptive by oversimplification and omission.

The best story without a well-matched, attentive audience can't win.

In sales, the best story without a well-matched, attentive audience with the willingness and ability to buy, to buy at your prices, and to buy now can't win.

And so on.

It's complicated.

In this book, you have gotten our best efforts at simplifying *some of* what's complicated about success in the marketplace and the marketplace of ideas. Although it was principally about the conveyance of story—the presentation and its all-important structure—we also provided experience-based insights on presenting on stages, in meeting rooms and by media. I want to acknowledge, though, that we have dealt with only a middle piece of a total success process. A great deal of success or failure with a presentation has to do with everything occurring with the audience before they ever see the presentation. Another major contributor to success or failure is everything occurring after the presentation. To use a trendy term, the presentation needs to occur inside a closed, controlled *ecosystem* you build, own, and control.

If you happen to already have that in place, you will be able to immediately go into it: to the places where you already have presentations in use and to places where there is opportunity to use presentations realized by reading this book and do profitable things immediately.

If you do not have such an ecosystem, then we have given you a start point and very good reasons to start, get smart, get busy, and build one. I make no apology for taking you to a Starting Line instead of carrying you across a Finish Line. After all, it is going to be *your* success.

I'll close with a story . . .

On a dark and stormy night, a very young man—a writer for an obscure, small-town publication—sat in the library of a home of one of the richest men then alive in the world: a baron of industry named Andrew Carnegie. A fire in the fireplace warmed the room. The young man interviewed the industrialist about his success and impressed Carnegie with his probative questions. They were different than the commonly asked questions. Instead of focusing on how rich he was, what he had done, and—often—being implicitly skeptical or critical about the economic injustice caused by his wealth, this young fellow was interested in why and how he had risen from nothing to his wealth and power. Carnegie had long nursed a pet idea—that success could be codified and taught just as mechanical engineering could. He envisioned a course or encyclopedia, a masterwork of some sort—the manual. On impulse, he presented this idea to his interviewer, along with a proposition: if the young writer would take on this project, Carnegie would use his influence to get the writer meetings with all the greatest achievers, entrepreneurs, industrialists, and inventors so that he could unearth and document the principles of thought and behavior these great men and women shared and adhered to—the secret "laws of success" they operated by that others did not. Carnegie said he would not financially subsidize the project, but he would retain no rights to it either. He asked for a decision. Unbeknownst to the young writer, Carnegie had a pocket watch held beneath his desk, and intended allowing a scant 60 seconds for the boy to prove decisive—or to fail that test. Napoleon Hill said yes, and 10 years later, in 1936, his encyclopedia, *Laws of Success,* and in 1937, his summary book, *Think and Grow Rich,* were published.

*Think and Grow Rich* has sold tens of millions of copies, reigned supreme as the most famous success book to this day, and continues to sell well absent any advertising or promotion all these years later. It's a good and worthy book. But without the story about it that I just told, it is just one of thousands of how-to-succeed books. New ones are published and promoted every year. Celebrities write them, powerful CEOs write them, ministers write them, academics write them, and people like me write them. Hill outperforms us all—because of the unique and compelling origin story behind the book.

Hill went on to a good career as a speaker, seminar leader, author of a number of other books, and for a time, a celebrity able to collect appearance fees just for being at a meeting, somewhat like a Kardashian gets paid just to hang out in a nightclub. He developed a number of powerful presentations as a paid lecturer.

Many, many years later, a man whose name you may know, Robert Kiyosaki, followed the Napoleon Hill blueprint and made himself valuably famous with a single story about his "rich dad, poor dad"—also his book's title.

My own business life has been largely made by a handful of stories told consistently for 30 to 40 years.

Back in 1992, by the way, there are records in TV and print interviews of a brash fellow telling a certain story about himself and telling a story about his frustrations with America losing, being taken advantage of, and needing to start winning again. Twenty-four years later, telling that same story, he won the Presidency of the United States. This year, he had an ecosystem for it, an organized way to use it, and a powerful presentation crafted around it.

Kiyosaki made a real business out of his story. Napoleon Hill didn't, and his later years were not secured by wealth despite all the fame he had created.

I put my stories into well-crafted presentations and have used those presentations to create an ecosystem I own and control. I kept putting new presentations into that ecosystem, and I became wealthy by doing so.

This is the point I want to leave you with: What you do with a powerful presentation is at least as important as having it in the first place.

# CHAPTER 18

# How to Fuel a Business with
## Effective Presentations
### Case History

by Mike Crow

I f you're like me, you're always looking for new or better ways to grow your business and to find a competitive edge in your market. If the reason you bought this book was more narrow and specific—maybe you had a looming need to deliver some sort of presentation, for example—I imagine you're happy to discover the topic is bigger than that. This is also a book about marketing and growing businesses. Also, if you're like me, you've seen and heard and been sold a lot of ideas that turn out to be a little thin, so you may be skeptical about how much impact using effective presentations can really have on your business. Doing so has certainly helped mine.

## $52+ Million Businesses with the Same Fuel

As the founder of the Millionaire Home Inspector community, I've developed many different strategies and methods for the thousands of independent home inspectors and owners of home inspection companies who follow my lead, based on my own outsized success at building a multimillion dollar a year company in this industry—twice. Within the association I created, I've helped over 50 of these small service businesses top the million dollar mark, a very high mark in our industry. Of all the strategies that I provide to them, I think making effective presentation to groups of real estate agents and others who can refer business to the inspectors is the most powerful and affordable. Fortunately for home inspectors, most real estate offices have agent meetings and the managers are usually open to having an outside speaker, so most of the inspectors who use my methods for this are doing in-office, small group presentations and can, if they are willing, do a lot of them.

Although all businesses can be different in different ways, Dan Kennedy is still correct when he says that no business is different. Every business needs customers, and every business has some type of connector persons who can be gathered into groups or who already gather into groups. My definition of a Connector is a trusted expert, influencer, or advisor who serves the customers or clients you want. Often, the Connector is the first point of contact from which a number of purchases flow.

For the home inspector, the best Connector is the real estate agent. No one can buy or sell a house without getting a home inspection done, but much more often than not, the real estate agent is the first person to deal with the customer, and that agent, by his or her recommendations, can control the home inspector used, the mortgage lender used, and the title company used. This means that agent can refer to the home inspector again and again and again. Every business has similar networks of connectors. For example, personal injury attorneys are the equivalent of real-estate agents to a chiropractor,. For the wedding photographer, it may be that the managers of wedding sites—hotels, resorts, special destinations—are Connectors. I don't know who the Connectors are for your business but I do know that whatever your business is, there is undoubtedly a group of Connectors.

It is obvious that having good working relationships with a number of Connectors can be great for your business. It can be a stabilizing force, leveling out the ups and downs of getting new customers by way of your own direct efforts or advertising. It can speed up growth without requiring a lot of money to invest in advertising or marketing. On the other hand, not having good relationships with Connectors can have them blocking business from coming to you, no matter how much you spend on advertising and how known you are in your market. They can also be deal killers, diverting customers away from you and into the hands of your competitor. For all these reasons, establishing relationships with Connectors is important. This is more important than many business owners think.

## Why Don't You Already Have a Great Circle of Connectors Bringing You all the New Customers You Can Handle?

The problem standing in the way of maximizing your relationships is that there are also pre-existing relationships between every Connector and your competitors. To start getting a stream of referrals from a Connector, you have to disrupt that relationship. I find the best way and definitely the most efficient way to do that is to get the opportunity to speak to a group of them. You get a certain lift of status by doing so, and you get an opportunity to demonstrate that you may be superior in some ways to the provider to whom they currently refer business. If pursuing the Connectors individually, one on one, you may get rejected a lot. You may be told, "I'm already working with someone. Thanks but no thanks." But imagine what might happen when that same Connector is in an audience of peers, and you appear as a speaker delivering an effective presentation. His hasty "no thanks" can convert into a "yes."

You need several things to win over a Connector. First, you need visibility. They have to know you exist and know what you do. Second, you need authority or credibility. You need trustworthiness. They have to know you are capable and competent, and worthy of referrals of their clients. Third, you need preference, reasons to favor you over other providers of the same or similar services. To get to this, you need opportunity! That's where getting invited in to speak to a group of Connectors comes in.

In my other business, Coach Blueprint, a company that supports business coaches in every field, I have cultivated relationships with the top Connectors in information marketing, speaking and coaching, including GKIC and Dan Kennedy. Either I or my daughter, Christa Trantham, who runs all three of our companies, makes a point of speaking at almost every GKIC event, by invitation or by sponsorship of a special session. I do for that business what I urge home inspectors to do for theirs: provide visibility, authority and preference.

## Stop Networking Start Connecting, with Connectors

In her book *The Connectors*, Maribeth Kuzmeski says, "Stop networking. Start connecting."

This is a powerful idea. Networking is random. It can take up a lot of time and make you feel like you're working hard and doing a lot, but it may not be very productive. Becoming known to and forming relationships with Connectors is not the same as ordinary networking. It is more focused.

You have a business to run. The home inspectors we coach are often running "mom 'n pop" small businesses. They may be owners, operators and still, also, doing inspections themselves. For them, for me, and for you, it's important to avoid low reward, time-eating activities. There's no shortage of things you might do to promote your business, so you have to be choosy. You ultimately want leverage, not just random exposure. When you connect with Connectors, you get leverage. Each one may be able to provide four, eight, 12, or 24 clients a year to a home inspector. I don't think there is any better way to make this happen than by delivering effective presentations to groups of Connectors.

## How to Get Positive Results with Audiences of Connectors

Obviously, this book in our hands is rich with advice about creating your presentation or presentations. I've learned a lot from Dan and from Dustin. You will too.

Here, I'm going to share some of the key pieces of advice I and my team of coaches give to the home inspectors about connecting with audiences. You'll have to do a bit of translation for your type of business, but a lot of it is easily adapted.

- *Offer useful, benefit-driven presentations,* not just a thinly veiled sales pitch. To be invited in to do a presentation and to have the agents feel good about it, it must actually add value to the meeting. We teach our home inspectors to assemble information and ideas that can be genuinely useful to the real estate agents. Most agents, like most other sales professionals and business owners, are very busy, poor time managers, and don't read or process as much information about their businesses as they should. It frankly doesn't take rocket science for a home inspector to collect and organize some up-to-date information from ordinary news sources and trade journals about trends and strategies that agents can use. The same thing is probably true in your field. Don't let this feel like some difficult task that is beyond you.

- *Teach the inspectors to offer the sales manager a choice of presentations to choose from.* This is a simple but effective idea. It switches the manager's decision from "Yes" or "No" to "Gee, I wonder which one of these would be best?" This sets up the magic question: "Which one of these topics do you think your agents would like to hear about most?" The manager picks; the inspector says, "Great—when would you like to schedule that?"

  Some of the choices we offer are:

  - Nine Marketing Secrets of Top Producing Real Estate Agents
  - The Top 10 Real Estate Apps and How To Profit from Them
  - Never Let a Home Inspection Kill a Sale Again
  - 10 Ways to Get More Referrals Every Month

- *Don't just get in once—get invited back again and again.* It's important to notice that three of these four choices have nothing to do with home inspections. It's a common mistake to want to go in and deliver a big, fat commercial for your business. Do that, and you won't be invited back. If you do this as we teach, delivering valuable information, you will be invited to come back and do a different presentation. Imagine the power of doing a presentation every few months to the same group of Connectors! For the home inspectors we coach, we've developed over 20 different presentations they can rotate.

If you can become a regular fixture with a group of Connectors, you will get one, then another, then another referring to you over time.

- *Do this a lot.* Once you have presentations that work and the ability to deliver them, you want to leverage this to the max. I push the home inspectors we coach to average one presentation per week or, if they have full-time marketing persons, to get them up to two presentations every week. This activity alone can drive a business like a home inspection service to heights most inspectors don't even think possible.

- *Prepare for each office.* If you have an agent you are already doing business with, you should talk with him or her in advance about giving a brief testimonial. Try and know who's who, so you can recognize the leaders the rest of the pack follows by name and accomplishments. Take these opportunities seriously.

- *Worry, a little!* If attendance is voluntary and uncertain, deliver promotional flyers to the office to be distributed to all the agents several days to a week in advance. Do not take attendance or interest for granted. Earn it.

- *Never neglect your "commercial" within your presentation.* You should have a direct call to action, offering a handout they'll want, coupons or vouchers giving discounts to their customers, etc., to bring them to you. You are there to impress, inform and make friends, but you are also there to get business. Don't forget your purpose.

There are many kinds of fuel for business growth.

Most business owners think in terms of getting their customers directly, through advertising, marketing, and promotion, and ignore opportunities to get those customers brought to them one after another after another by Connectors. Establishing your own circle of Connectors can fuel your business like nothing else. The effective presentation can make that happen.

Mike Crow is the founder of Millionaire Home Inspector Community, which can be seen at http://homeinspectorblueprint.com. He is also President of CoachingBlueprint.com, providing training, ready-to-use tools and support for business coaches and consultants in every field.

# About the Authors

**DAN KENNEDY** is a serial entrepreneur who has started, bought, built, and sold businesses of various types and sizes—all driven by powerful presentations. He is a highly sought-after and outrageously well-paid direct-marketing consultant and direct-response copywriter, coach to groups of entrepreneurs and professionals, a nearly retired yet popular professional speaker, author, and, of all things, a professional harness racing driver. He lives with his second and third wife (same woman) and a small dog in Ohio and Virginia. His office that he never visits is in Phoenix. He can be reached directly only by fax at (602) 269-3113 or by mail at Kennedy Inner Circle, Inc., 15433 N. Tatum Blvd., #104, Phoenix, Arizona 85032. Do NOT email him at any websites presenting his information. They belong to publishers; he does not use email. Information about the membership organization focused around Dan's work, its online courses, resources, SuperConferences℠ and Info-SUMMITS℠ can be accessed at http://GKIC.com

**DUSTIN MATHEWS** is widely recognized as a direct-response marketer and for his *unique* ability to transform businesses and brands. Leveraging powerful presentations, Dustin assisted two different companies to get on the *Inc.* magazine's 500—a coveted list of fastest growing private companies in America.

Now he runs Speaking Empire, a disruptive company in the leadership training and education space. Along with multiple best-selling books in the areas of marketing, sales, and life, Dustin codified a process for creating and innovating in the area of Brand Response™.

Dustin Mathews and his latest findings can be found online at www.SpeakingEmpire.com and http://DustinMathews.com. You may reach him at (800) 687-4061 or by mail at 160 Sixth Street SW, Largo, FL 33770.

**DAVE VANHOOSE** is a master communicator, celebrity speaker trainer, and an Arena Bowl World Champion. In three years, he took his first company to number 35 on the *Inc. 500* list of fastest growing private companies in America. Leveraging powerful presentations, he grew the company to 100+ employees, over $30 million in revenue, and 50 to 100 seminar events per month!

Based on his *learned* ability to communicate effectively, Dave was invited as one of a few privileged speakers to the Get Motivated Success Tour along with past presidents and world leaders such as Bill Clinton, George Bush, Ronald Reagan, and

Mikhail Gorbachev; sports stars such as Michael Phelps and Joe Montana; and business personalities like Steve Forbes and Steve Wozniak.

With over 3,000 presentations delivered, Dave is now focusing on motivating world-class entrepreneurs and business owners to achieve more than they ever thought possible via powerful presentations.

Dave VanHoose can be reached at (800) 687-4061 or found online at www.SpeakingEmpire.com and http://DaveVanHoose.com.

## Other Books By Dan Kennedy

In the NO B.S. Series, published by Entrepreneur Press

*No B.S. DIRECT Marketing for NON-Direct Marketing Businesses, 2nd Edition*

*No B.S. Guide to Maximum Referrals & Customer Retention* with Shaun Buck

*No B.S. Guide to Direct-Response Social Media Marketing* with Kim Walsh-Phillips

*No B.S. Guide to Brand-Building by Direct Response*

*No B.S. Trust-Based Marketing* with Matt Zagula

*No B.S. Guide to Marketing to Leading-Edge Boomers and Seniors* with Chip Kessler

*No B.S. Price Strategy* with Jason Marrs

*No B.S. Marketing to the Affluent, 2nd Edition*

*No B.S. Ruthless Management of People & Profits, 2nd Edition*

*No B.S. Grassroots Marketing* with Jeff Slutsky

*No B.S. Business Success in the New Economy*

*No B.S. Sales Success in the New Economy*

*No B.S. Wealth Attraction in the New Economy*

*No B.S. Time Management for Entrepreneurs, 2nd Edition*

## *Other Books*

*Speak to Sell* (Advantage)

*Make 'Em Laugh & Take Their Money* (GKIC/Morgan-James)

*The Ultimate Sales Letter—4th Edition/20th Anniversary Edition* (Adams Media)

*The Ultimate Marketing Plan—4th Edition/20th Anniversary Edition* (Adams Media)

*Making Them Believe: 21 Principles and Lost Secrets of Dr. J.R. Brinkley-Style Marketing* with Chip Kessler (GKIC/ Morgan-James)

*My Unfinished Business/Autobiographical Essays* (Advantage)

*The NEW Psycho-Cybernetics* with Maxwell Maltz M.D. (Prentice-Hall)

# Index

strategy session webinars,
121–124

**B**

benefits of the benefits, 35–36

bigger reasons, 49, 137

Bleier, Rocky, 112

bonuses, 38, 43–44

boot camps, 76, 78–79, 80

buying ability, 91–92

buying now, 93–94

buying willingness, 92–94

**C**

calls to action, 38–39, 118, 154

campaigns, follow-up, 132–133

can they buy, 91–92

Carnegie, Andrew, 143–144

celebrity hosts, 112

chat boxes, 118

Clients on Demand, 121–124

competence, 11, 150

competitive advantage, x–xi,
149–150

components of presentations,
24

confidence, 11–12

connecting vs. networking,
150–151, 154

connector groups, presenting
to, 151–154

connectors, 148–154

contact information,
capturing, 102–103

conversion, 78, 117, 118, 121,
122, 134, 150

credibility, 11, 32–33, 46, 49,
150

Crow, Mike, 154

customer appreciation events,
75

**D**

deadlines, 37–38

definition of presentations, 24

delivery, 63

demonstrations, 67–72

direct hits, 14–15

direct-sale webinars, 124–126

discipline, 23

discounts, 38, 46–47, 138, 154

*Dynamic Selling* (Tralins), 4

dynamism, 65

**E**

effective presentation formula,
25, 30–39

effective presentation results,
5–6, 16, 87–94. *See also*
success with presentations

events, free vs. paid, 79–80

events, live. *See* live events

Evert, Chris, 112

excitement, building, 100–102

optimal times of day for,
78–79

planning, 76–79

targeting audiences for,
80–84

types of, 75–76

live vs. automated webinars,
120–122

local events, planning, 76–77

**M**

Magic Question List, 17–18

Magnetic Marketing System,
28

Marie, Rose, 112

marketing assets, 108

mass persuasion, 61–65

Mathews, Dustin, xv, 156

maximum-effectiveness
presentations, 24–25

McFarland, Packy, 110

mindset, pre-existing, 87–94

**N**

national-level events, 77

networking vs. connecting,
150–151

networks, 148–154

no-risk guarantees, 36–37

now-or-never discounts, 38

**O**

offers, 36, 41–42, 53–54.

*See also* Irresistible Offer
Architecture

one-to-many selling, 28–30, 74

online presentations, 99–105,
108–112. *See also* automated
webinars; demonstrations

online testimonials, 111

onsite workplace
presentations, xiii–xiv

opt-in pages, 102–103

outcomes, desired, 22, 24

over delivering, 104–105

overcoming fear, 10–12, 23

**P**

paid vs. free events, 79–80

pain, targeting, 33, 137

performance of presentations,
24

perpetual contrast, 47

persuasion, mass, 61–65

phone conversations, follow-
up, 134–139

planning live events, 76–79

post-presentation phone
conversations, 134–139

Powter, Susan, 110

pre-existing conditions, 87–94

pre-framing audience
reactions, 34–35

Presentainers, 62

presentations, definition of, 24

stories, 31, 141–145

strategy session webinars, 121–124

success with presentations, 85, 142. *See also* effective presentation results

**T**

targeting audiences, 80–84

teaching vs. delivering solutions, 33–34

telephone follow-up, 134–139

testimonials, 111

*Think and Grow Rich* (Hill), 144

3DMailResults, xii

time-limited discounts, 38

traffic generation, 99–100

transparency, 32

Trantham, Christa, 150

triggers, 17

Trump, Donald, ix, xv–xvi, 14, 15, 74

Trump rallies, x

trust, 32, 79, 122, 150

TV presentations, xiv–xv, 24, 108–113. *See also* infomercials

**U**

urgency, creating, 37–38

**V**

value, added, 44–47

value, building, 36

VanHoose, Dave, 156–157

venues for presentations, 97–98

video presentations, 109–112. *See also* TV presentations; webinars

video sales letters (VSL), xii, 28, 112

video testimonials, 111

videos, excitement-building, 110

visibility, 150

VSLs (video sales letters), xii, 28, 112

**W**

webcasts, 110

Webinar Formula, 99–105

webinar prosperity segmentation, 118–120

webinars, 99–105, 108–112

webinars, automated. *See* automated webinars

willingness to buy, 92–93

willingness to buy now, 93–94

**Y**

yes state, 63–64, 136

## Need Help With Your POWERFUL Presentation?

We believe that every entrepreneur has a message—and a powerful presentation inside. The challenge is most don't understand how to find that message and then structure it into a way that gets audiences in action.

Speaking Empire removes the stress of creating your own presentation. Imagine having:

- A complete presentation maximized for presenting live and virtually.

- An irresistible offer congruent with your positioning and branding that gets prospects into action.

- Our experts review your presentation before you deliver.

Discover why the word's most successful entrepreneurs call upon Speaking Empire to help them influence one to many. For the next event in your area call **800-687-4061** or go to **www.SpeakingEmpire.com**.

### DOES YOUR DELIVERY MOVE PEOPLE? IT SHOULD.

Who makes more money? A teacher or a Hollywood actor?

Deep down, people don't want to be trained, they want to be entertained.

A lot of folks believe in their products and services so much that they share too much too fast. What I mean by that is: they teach too much.

When you understand the principles of a Presentainer®, you'll maximize every communication with the world.

**For more information, visit www.SpeakingEmpire.com today or call 800-687-4061 for the next event in your area.**